50 Premium Greek Cooking Recipes for Home

By: Kelly Johnson

Table of Contents

- Spanakopita (Spinach Pie)
- Moussaka
- Souvlaki (Grilled Meat Skewers)
- Tzatziki Sauce
- Dolmades (Stuffed Grape Leaves)
- Greek Salad
- Baklava
- Fasolada (Bean Soup)
- Pastitsio
- Keftedes (Greek Meatballs)
- Avgolemono Soup (Egg-Lemon Soup)
- Koulourakia (Greek Butter Cookies)
- Galaktoboureko (Custard Pastry)
- Loukoumades (Greek Honey Puffs)
- Tiropita (Cheese Pie)
- Greek Lemon Potatoes
- Revani (Semolina Cake)
- Stifado (Greek Beef Stew)
- Melitzanosalata (Eggplant Dip)
- Gyro Sandwich
- Kleftiko (Greek Lamb)
- Gemista (Stuffed Vegetables)
- Saganaki (Fried Cheese)
- Yemista (Stuffed Bell Peppers)
- Greek Yogurt with Honey and Nuts
- Psarosoupa (Fish Soup)
- Melomakarona (Honey Cookies)
- Greek Chicken with Orzo
- Karidopita (Walnut Cake)
- Kalamata Olive Bread
- Kolokithopita (Zucchini Pie)
- Pasteli (Sesame Seed and Honey Bars)
- Pitarakia (Fried Dough Pastries)
- Octopus in Red Wine
- Kadaifi (Shredded Phyllo Pastry)
- Keftedakia (Greek Meatballs)

- Melitzanes Papoutsakia (Stuffed Eggplants)
- Bougatsa (Cream-Filled Pastry)
- Arni Lemonato (Lemon Garlic Lamb)
- Loukoumades (Greek Donuts)
- Taramosalata (Fish Roe Dip)
- Strapatsada (Scrambled Eggs with Tomatoes)
- Dakos (Cretan Salad)
- Karidopita (Walnut Cake)
- Souvlakia (Skewers with Lamb or Chicken)
- Moussaka (Eggplant Casserole)
- Spanakopita (Spinach Pie)
- Avgolemono (Egg-Lemon Chicken Soup)
- Fasolada (Bean Soup)
- Baklava

Spanakopita (Spinach Pie)

Ingredients:

- 1 package (16 oz) frozen chopped spinach, thawed and drained
- 1 cup crumbled feta cheese
- 1 cup ricotta cheese
- 1/2 cup grated Parmesan cheese
- 1/2 cup chopped green onions (or 1 small onion, finely chopped)
- 2 cloves garlic, minced
- 1/4 cup chopped fresh dill (or 1 tablespoon dried dill)
- 1/4 cup chopped fresh parsley
- 2 eggs, lightly beaten
- Salt and pepper, to taste
- 1/2 cup (1 stick) unsalted butter, melted
- 1 package (16 oz) phyllo dough, thawed according to package instructions
- Olive oil (for brushing)

Instructions:

1. **Prepare the Filling:**
    - Preheat your oven to 350°F (175°C).
    - In a large bowl, combine the drained spinach, feta cheese, ricotta cheese, Parmesan cheese, green onions, garlic, dill, parsley, eggs, salt, and pepper. Mix well until all ingredients are evenly incorporated.
2. **Assemble the Spanakopita:**
    - Unroll the phyllo dough sheets on a clean, dry surface and cover them with a damp kitchen towel to prevent drying out.
    - Brush a 9x13 inch baking dish with melted butter.
    - Place one sheet of phyllo dough into the baking dish and brush lightly with melted butter. Repeat this process, layering about 10 sheets of phyllo dough, brushing each layer with butter.
3. **Add the Filling:**
    - Spread the spinach and cheese filling evenly over the layered phyllo dough in the baking dish.
4. **Finish Layering:**
    - Continue layering the remaining phyllo dough sheets on top of the filling, brushing each sheet with melted butter. Fold any excess dough from the edges over the top layer.
5. **Bake:**
    - Brush the top layer generously with olive oil. Using a sharp knife, score the top layer into squares or triangles, being careful not to cut all the way through to the filling.

- Bake in the preheated oven for 45-55 minutes, or until the top is golden brown and crispy.
6. **Serve:**
    - Remove from the oven and let it cool for a few minutes before slicing along the scored lines and serving warm.

Spanakopita is delicious served as an appetizer, side dish, or even as a light main course with a fresh Greek salad. Enjoy!

Moussaka

Ingredients:

For the Eggplant Layers:

- 2-3 large eggplants, sliced into 1/4 inch rounds
- Salt
- Olive oil, for brushing

For the Meat Sauce:

- 1 lb ground lamb or beef
- 1 onion, finely chopped
- 2 cloves garlic, minced
- 1 can (14 oz) diced tomatoes
- 2 tbsp tomato paste
- 1 tsp dried oregano
- 1/2 tsp ground cinnamon
- Salt and pepper, to taste
- Olive oil, for cooking

For the Béchamel Sauce:

- 1/2 cup unsalted butter
- 1/2 cup all-purpose flour
- 4 cups milk
- Salt and pepper, to taste
- 1/4 tsp ground nutmeg
- 2 eggs, beaten
- 1/2 cup grated Parmesan cheese

Instructions:

1. **Prepare the Eggplant:**
    - Place the eggplant slices on a baking sheet lined with paper towels. Sprinkle salt over both sides of the slices and let them sit for about 30 minutes to draw out moisture. Pat dry with paper towels.
    - Preheat the oven to 400°F (200°C). Brush the eggplant slices lightly with olive oil and arrange them on baking sheets. Bake for 15-20 minutes until tender. Set aside.
2. **Make the Meat Sauce:**
    - Heat a drizzle of olive oil in a large skillet over medium heat. Add the chopped onion and garlic, sauté until softened.

- Add the ground lamb or beef to the skillet, breaking it up with a spoon. Cook until browned.
- Stir in the diced tomatoes, tomato paste, oregano, cinnamon, salt, and pepper. Simmer for about 15-20 minutes until the sauce thickens. Remove from heat and set aside.

3. **Prepare the Béchamel Sauce:**
    - In a saucepan, melt the butter over medium heat. Add the flour and whisk continuously for 1-2 minutes until smooth and bubbly.
    - Gradually whisk in the milk, a little at a time, until smooth and thickened. Season with salt, pepper, and nutmeg. Cook for another 2-3 minutes, stirring constantly.
    - Remove the saucepan from heat. Allow the béchamel sauce to cool slightly, then whisk in the beaten eggs and grated Parmesan cheese until smooth. Set aside.

4. **Assemble the Moussaka:**
    - Preheat the oven to 375°F (190°C).
    - Grease a large baking dish (about 9x13 inches) with olive oil. Arrange half of the eggplant slices in a single layer on the bottom of the dish.
    - Spread half of the meat sauce evenly over the eggplant layer.
    - Layer the remaining eggplant slices on top, followed by the remaining meat sauce.
    - Pour the béchamel sauce evenly over the top, spreading it with a spatula to cover the entire surface.

5. **Bake the Moussaka:**
    - Place the moussaka in the preheated oven and bake for 45-55 minutes, or until the top is golden brown and bubbly.
    - Remove from the oven and let it rest for 15-20 minutes before slicing and serving.

6. **Serve:**
    - Moussaka is best served warm. Cut into squares and enjoy this comforting and hearty Greek dish!

Moussaka pairs well with a fresh Greek salad and crusty bread. It's a delicious and satisfying meal that's perfect for gatherings or special occasions.

Souvlaki (Grilled Meat Skewers)

Ingredients:

For the Marinade:

- 1.5 lbs (about 700g) boneless meat (pork, chicken breast, or lamb), cut into 1-inch cubes
- 1/4 cup olive oil
- 1/4 cup lemon juice
- 3 cloves garlic, minced
- 1 tsp dried oregano
- 1 tsp dried thyme
- 1/2 tsp paprika
- Salt and pepper, to taste

For Serving:

- Pita bread or flatbread
- Tzatziki sauce (recipe below)
- Sliced tomatoes
- Sliced onions
- Chopped fresh parsley (optional)

Instructions:

1. **Prepare the Marinade:**
   - In a bowl, whisk together olive oil, lemon juice, minced garlic, oregano, thyme, paprika, salt, and pepper.
2. **Marinate the Meat:**
   - Place the cubed meat in a shallow dish or resealable plastic bag. Pour the marinade over the meat, ensuring all pieces are coated evenly. Cover or seal and refrigerate for at least 1 hour, preferably longer (up to overnight) for best flavor.
3. **Skewer the Meat:**
   - If using wooden skewers, soak them in water for at least 30 minutes to prevent burning.
   - Thread the marinated meat onto skewers, leaving a small space between each piece.
4. **Grill the Souvlaki:**
   - Preheat your grill to medium-high heat.
   - Place the skewers on the grill and cook for about 10-12 minutes, turning occasionally, until the meat is cooked through and nicely charred on all sides.
5. **Serve:**
   - Remove the skewers from the grill and let them rest for a few minutes.
   - Serve the souvlaki on pita bread or flatbread, topped with tzatziki sauce, sliced tomatoes, onions, and chopped parsley if desired.

Tzatziki Sauce:

Ingredients:

- 1 cup Greek yogurt
- 1/2 cucumber, grated and squeezed to remove excess moisture
- 2 cloves garlic, minced
- 1 tbsp olive oil
- 1 tbsp lemon juice
- 1 tbsp chopped fresh dill (or 1 tsp dried dill)
- Salt and pepper, to taste

Instructions:

1. In a bowl, combine Greek yogurt, grated cucumber, minced garlic, olive oil, lemon juice, and chopped dill. Mix well.
2. Season with salt and pepper to taste. Adjust consistency with a little water if necessary.
3. Chill in the refrigerator for at least 30 minutes before serving to allow flavors to blend.

Enjoy your homemade souvlaki with freshly made tzatziki sauce and your favorite Mediterranean sides for a delicious and satisfying meal!

Tzatziki Sauce

Ingredients:

- 1 cup Greek yogurt (preferably full-fat)
- 1/2 cucumber, grated
- 2 cloves garlic, minced
- 1 tbsp olive oil
- 1 tbsp lemon juice (or white wine vinegar)
- 1 tbsp chopped fresh dill (or 1 tsp dried dill)
- Salt and pepper, to taste

Instructions:

1. **Prepare the Cucumber:**
    - Grate the cucumber using a box grater. Place the grated cucumber in a fine-mesh sieve or cheesecloth and squeeze out excess moisture. Alternatively, you can squeeze the grated cucumber with your hands over the sink to remove water.
2. **Mix Ingredients:**
    - In a bowl, combine the Greek yogurt, grated cucumber, minced garlic, olive oil, lemon juice (or vinegar), and chopped dill.
3. **Season:**
    - Season with salt and pepper to taste. Be cautious with the salt as the yogurt can be salty already.
4. **Chill:**
    - Cover the bowl and refrigerate the tzatziki sauce for at least 30 minutes before serving. This allows the flavors to meld together.
5. **Serve:**
    - Stir the tzatziki sauce before serving. Drizzle with a little extra olive oil and garnish with a sprig of fresh dill if desired.
    - Serve tzatziki sauce as a dip with pita bread, fresh vegetables, or alongside grilled meats like souvlaki or gyros.

Tzatziki sauce can be stored in an airtight container in the refrigerator for up to 3-4 days. It's a versatile and delicious addition to Mediterranean-inspired dishes, adding a cool and creamy element with a burst of flavor from the garlic, dill, and cucumber. Enjoy!

Dolmades (Stuffed Grape Leaves)

Ingredients:

For the Grape Leaves:

- 1 jar (about 8 oz) grape leaves in brine, rinsed and drained
- Water, for boiling

For the Filling:

- 1 cup long-grain rice
- 1/2 cup finely chopped onion
- 1/4 cup chopped fresh dill
- 1/4 cup chopped fresh parsley
- 1/4 cup pine nuts or chopped almonds (optional)
- 1/4 cup olive oil
- Juice of 1 lemon
- Salt and pepper, to taste

For Cooking:

- 1-2 cups vegetable or chicken broth (or water)
- Juice of 1-2 lemons
- Olive oil, for drizzling

Instructions:

1. **Prepare the Grape Leaves:**
    - Rinse the grape leaves under cold water to remove excess saltiness from the brine. Place them in a bowl and cover with boiling water. Let them soak for about 5-10 minutes to soften. Drain and set aside.
2. **Prepare the Filling:**
    - In a bowl, combine the rice, chopped onion, dill, parsley, pine nuts (if using), olive oil, lemon juice, salt, and pepper. Mix well until all ingredients are evenly incorporated.
3. **Assemble the Dolmades:**
    - Lay a grape leaf flat on a work surface, shiny side down, with the stem facing you. Trim off any tough stems.
    - Place about 1 tablespoon of the rice filling near the stem end of the grape leaf. Fold the bottom of the leaf over the filling, then fold in the sides, and roll tightly into a cylinder shape.
    - Repeat with the remaining grape leaves and filling mixture, placing the dolmades seam-side down in a large pot or deep skillet.
4. **Cook the Dolmades:**

- Arrange the dolmades snugly in the pot in layers. Pour enough vegetable or chicken broth (or water) over them to just cover.
- Place a heatproof plate upside down on top of the dolmades to keep them submerged while cooking.
- Bring to a boil over medium-high heat, then reduce the heat to low, cover, and simmer for about 45-60 minutes, or until the rice is fully cooked and tender.

5. **Finish and Serve:**
   - Once cooked, carefully remove the dolmades from the pot using a slotted spoon and arrange them on a serving platter.
   - Drizzle with additional olive oil and lemon juice over the dolmades.
   - Serve dolmades warm or at room temperature as an appetizer or part of a mezze platter.

Dolmades can be enjoyed on their own or with a side of tzatziki sauce. They are deliciously tangy and aromatic, making them a favorite in Mediterranean cuisine.

Greek Salad

Ingredients:

- 4-5 ripe tomatoes, cut into wedges or chunks
- 1 cucumber, sliced
- 1 red onion, thinly sliced
- 1 green bell pepper, seeded and sliced
- 1/2 cup Kalamata olives, pitted
- 1/2 cup feta cheese, crumbled
- Fresh oregano leaves, chopped (optional, for garnish)

For the Dressing:

- 1/4 cup extra virgin olive oil
- 2 tbsp red wine vinegar
- 1-2 cloves garlic, minced
- 1 tsp dried oregano
- Salt and pepper, to taste

Instructions:

1. **Prepare the Vegetables:**
   - In a large salad bowl, combine the tomatoes, cucumber, red onion, and bell pepper.
2. **Add Olives and Feta:**
   - Scatter the Kalamata olives and crumbled feta cheese over the vegetables.
3. **Make the Dressing:**
   - In a small bowl, whisk together the olive oil, red wine vinegar, minced garlic, dried oregano, salt, and pepper until well combined.
4. **Assemble the Salad:**
   - Drizzle the dressing over the salad ingredients in the bowl.
5. **Toss Gently:**
   - Gently toss the salad to coat everything evenly with the dressing.
6. **Garnish and Serve:**
   - Garnish the Greek salad with fresh oregano leaves, if desired.
   - Serve immediately as a side dish or as a main course with crusty bread.

Tips:

- For a twist, you can add some chopped fresh parsley or mint leaves to the salad.
- Adjust the amount of dressing according to your taste preferences. Some like it with a bit more tang from the vinegar, while others prefer a milder dressing.
- Serve the Greek salad chilled or at room temperature.

Enjoy this colorful and flavorful Greek salad as a light and healthy addition to any meal, or as part of a Mediterranean-inspired spread!

Baklava

Ingredients:

For the Baklava:

- 1 package (16 oz) phyllo dough, thawed according to package instructions
- 1 cup unsalted butter, melted
- 2 cups nuts (walnuts, pistachios, almonds), finely chopped
- 1 tsp ground cinnamon
- 1/4 tsp ground cloves
- 1 cup granulated sugar

For the Syrup:

- 1 cup water
- 1 cup granulated sugar
- 1/2 cup honey
- 1 cinnamon stick (optional)
- 1 tsp vanilla extract
- Zest of 1 lemon or orange (optional)

Instructions:

1. **Prepare the Syrup:**
   - In a saucepan, combine water, sugar, honey, cinnamon stick (if using), vanilla extract, and citrus zest (if using). Bring to a boil over medium-high heat, stirring occasionally. Reduce heat and simmer for 10 minutes. Remove from heat and let the syrup cool completely. Once cooled, remove the cinnamon stick and citrus zest.
2. **Prepare the Nuts:**
   - In a food processor, pulse the nuts until finely chopped. Alternatively, you can chop them by hand with a sharp knife.
3. **Prepare the Baklava Layers:**
   - Preheat your oven to 350°F (175°C). Butter a 9x13 inch baking dish.
   - Place one sheet of phyllo dough in the baking dish and brush lightly with melted butter. Repeat this process, layering about 10 sheets of phyllo dough, brushing each layer with butter.
4. **Add the Nut Filling:**
   - Sprinkle a generous amount of the chopped nuts evenly over the buttered phyllo layers. Sprinkle with cinnamon, cloves, and sugar.
5. **Continue Layering:**
   - Continue layering the remaining phyllo sheets on top of the nut mixture, brushing each sheet with melted butter. Make sure to brush the top layer generously with butter.

6. **Cut and Bake:**
     - Using a sharp knife, cut the baklava into diamond or square shapes all the way to the bottom of the dish.
     - Bake in the preheated oven for 50-60 minutes, or until the baklava is golden brown and crispy.
7. **Pour Syrup Over Baklava:**
     - Remove the baklava from the oven and immediately pour the cooled syrup evenly over the hot baklava. Allow it to absorb the syrup and cool completely in the dish on a wire rack.
8. **Serve:**
     - Once cooled, cut through the pre-cut lines all the way to the bottom again and serve.

Baklava is best stored at room temperature, covered with foil or plastic wrap, and can be kept for several days. It's a wonderful dessert to enjoy with a cup of coffee or tea, and it makes a beautiful addition to any dessert table or special occasion!

Fasolada (Bean Soup)

Ingredients:

- 1 cup dried white beans (such as Great Northern beans or cannellini beans), soaked overnight
- 2-3 tbsp olive oil
- 1 onion, finely chopped
- 2-3 cloves garlic, minced
- 2 carrots, diced
- 2 celery stalks, diced
- 1 can (14 oz) diced tomatoes
- 1 tbsp tomato paste
- 1 bay leaf
- 1 tsp dried oregano
- Salt and pepper, to taste
- Water or vegetable broth, as needed
- Fresh parsley, chopped, for garnish
- Crusty bread, for serving

Instructions:

1. **Prepare the Beans:**
   - Rinse the soaked beans and drain them. Place them in a large pot and cover with fresh water. Bring to a boil, then reduce the heat and simmer for about 30-40 minutes, or until the beans are tender. Drain and set aside.
2. **Saute the Vegetables:**
   - In a large soup pot or Dutch oven, heat the olive oil over medium heat. Add the chopped onion and cook until softened, about 5 minutes.
   - Add the minced garlic, diced carrots, and diced celery. Cook for another 5 minutes, stirring occasionally.
3. **Add Tomatoes and Seasonings:**
   - Stir in the diced tomatoes, tomato paste, bay leaf, dried oregano, salt, and pepper. Cook for a few minutes to combine the flavors.
4. **Simmer the Soup:**
   - Add the cooked beans to the pot. Pour in enough water or vegetable broth to cover the ingredients (about 4-6 cups).
   - Bring the soup to a boil, then reduce the heat to low. Cover and simmer for 30-40 minutes, stirring occasionally, until the vegetables are tender and the flavors have melded together.
5. **Adjust Seasoning and Serve:**
   - Taste and adjust seasoning with more salt and pepper if needed.
   - Remove the bay leaf before serving.

- Ladle the fasolada into bowls. Garnish with chopped fresh parsley and serve hot with crusty bread on the side.

Tips:

- You can add a splash of red wine vinegar or lemon juice at the end to brighten the flavors of the soup.
- Fasolada is often enjoyed with a drizzle of olive oil on top and a sprinkle of crumbled feta cheese.
- This soup gets even better the next day as the flavors continue to develop. Store any leftovers in the refrigerator for up to 3-4 days.

Fasolada is a comforting and satisfying dish, perfect for cooler weather or anytime you crave a wholesome bowl of soup. Enjoy this taste of Greek culinary tradition!

Pastitsio

Ingredients:

For the Meat Sauce:

- 1 lb ground beef or lamb
- 1 onion, finely chopped
- 2 cloves garlic, minced
- 1 can (14 oz) crushed tomatoes
- 2 tbsp tomato paste
- 1/2 cup red wine (optional)
- 1 tsp dried oregano
- 1/2 tsp ground cinnamon
- 1/4 tsp ground cloves
- Salt and pepper, to taste
- Olive oil, for cooking

For the Pasta:

- 1 lb penne or macaroni pasta
- Salt, for cooking pasta
- Olive oil, for tossing pasta

For the Béchamel Sauce:

- 6 tbsp unsalted butter
- 1/2 cup all-purpose flour
- 4 cups milk
- 1/4 tsp ground nutmeg
- Salt and pepper, to taste
- 2 eggs, lightly beaten
- 1 cup grated Parmesan cheese

Instructions:

1. **Prepare the Pasta:**
   - Cook the pasta in a large pot of salted boiling water according to package instructions until al dente. Drain and toss with a little olive oil to prevent sticking. Set aside.
2. **Make the Meat Sauce:**
   - In a large skillet or saucepan, heat olive oil over medium-high heat. Add the chopped onion and cook until softened, about 5 minutes.
   - Add the minced garlic and ground meat to the skillet. Cook, breaking up the meat with a spoon, until browned.

- Stir in the crushed tomatoes, tomato paste, red wine (if using), oregano, cinnamon, cloves, salt, and pepper. Simmer for about 20-30 minutes until the sauce thickens. Remove from heat and set aside.

3. **Prepare the Béchamel Sauce:**
    - In a medium saucepan, melt the butter over medium heat. Stir in the flour and cook, stirring constantly, for 1-2 minutes until smooth and bubbly.
    - Gradually whisk in the milk, a little at a time, until smooth and thickened. Cook for another 5-7 minutes, stirring constantly, until the sauce coats the back of a spoon.
    - Season with nutmeg, salt, and pepper. Remove from heat and let it cool slightly.
    - Gradually whisk in the beaten eggs and grated Parmesan cheese until smooth and well combined. Set aside.
4. **Assemble the Pastitsio:**
    - Preheat your oven to 350°F (175°C). Butter a 9x13 inch baking dish.
    - Spread half of the cooked pasta evenly on the bottom of the baking dish.
    - Spread the meat sauce evenly over the pasta layer.
    - Top with the remaining pasta, spreading it evenly.
5. **Add the Béchamel Sauce:**
    - Pour the béchamel sauce evenly over the top pasta layer, spreading it with a spatula to cover the entire surface.
6. **Bake the Pastitsio:**
    - Place the baking dish in the preheated oven and bake for 45-55 minutes, or until the top is golden brown and bubbly.
7. **Serve:**
    - Remove from the oven and let it rest for 15-20 minutes before slicing and serving.

Pastitsio is often served warm as a main dish, accompanied by a fresh Greek salad and crusty bread. It's a comforting and flavorful dish that's perfect for gatherings or special occasions. Enjoy your homemade pastitsio!

Keftedes (Greek Meatballs)

Ingredients:

For the Meatballs:

- 1 lb ground beef
- 1/2 lb ground pork (or use all beef if preferred)
- 1 onion, finely chopped or grated
- 2 cloves garlic, minced
- 1/2 cup breadcrumbs
- 1/4 cup chopped fresh parsley
- 1/4 cup chopped fresh mint (or 1 tbsp dried mint)
- 1 tsp dried oregano
- 1/2 tsp ground cumin
- 1/4 tsp ground cinnamon
- Salt and pepper, to taste
- 1 egg, lightly beaten
- Olive oil, for frying

For Serving:

- Tzatziki sauce (see previous recipe for instructions)

Instructions:

1. **Prepare the Meatball Mixture:**
   - In a large bowl, combine the ground beef, ground pork, chopped onion, minced garlic, breadcrumbs, parsley, mint, oregano, cumin, cinnamon, salt, pepper, and beaten egg. Mix well using your hands until all ingredients are evenly incorporated.
2. **Shape the Meatballs:**
   - Take small portions of the meat mixture and roll them into balls about 1-1.5 inches in diameter. Place them on a plate or baking sheet lined with parchment paper.
3. **Cook the Keftedes:**
   - In a large skillet, heat enough olive oil over medium-high heat to cover the bottom of the pan.
   - Working in batches to avoid overcrowding, carefully place the meatballs in the hot oil. Cook for about 3-4 minutes per side, or until they are browned and cooked through. Use a spatula to gently turn them to ensure even cooking.
   - Remove the cooked keftedes from the skillet and place them on a plate lined with paper towels to absorb excess oil.
4. **Serve:**
   - Arrange the keftedes on a serving platter.

        - Serve hot with tzatziki sauce on the side for dipping or drizzling.
  5. **Optional:**
        - Garnish with additional chopped fresh herbs, such as parsley or mint, for added freshness and flavor.

Keftedes are perfect as an appetizer, part of a meze platter, or as a main course served with rice, salad, or grilled vegetables. They are flavorful, tender, and make a delightful addition to any Greek-inspired meal. Enjoy your homemade keftedes!

Avgolemono Soup (Egg-Lemon Soup)

Ingredients:

- 8 cups chicken broth (homemade or low-sodium store-bought)
- 1/2 cup Arborio rice or long-grain white rice
- 3 eggs
- Juice of 2-3 lemons (about 1/2 to 3/4 cup)
- Salt and pepper, to taste
- Chopped fresh dill, for garnish (optional)

Instructions:

1. **Cook the Rice:**
    - In a large pot, bring the chicken broth to a boil. Add the rice and reduce heat to medium-low. Simmer for about 15-20 minutes, or until the rice is cooked and tender.
2. **Prepare the Avgolemono Mixture:**
    - In a bowl, whisk together the eggs and lemon juice until well combined.
3. **Temper the Eggs:**
    - Take a ladleful of the hot broth from the pot and slowly pour it into the egg-lemon mixture, whisking constantly. This step helps to temper the eggs so they do not curdle when added to the hot soup.
4. **Add the Avgolemono Mixture to the Soup:**
    - Gradually pour the tempered egg-lemon mixture back into the pot of hot broth and rice, stirring gently to combine. Heat the soup over low heat, stirring constantly, for a few minutes until slightly thickened. Do not let it boil once the eggs are added to prevent curdling.
5. **Season and Serve:**
    - Season the Avgolemono soup with salt and pepper to taste.
    - Ladle the soup into bowls and garnish with chopped fresh dill, if desired.

Tips:

- The consistency of Avgolemono soup can be adjusted by varying the amount of rice used or by adding more or less lemon juice according to your taste preference.
- For a heartier version, you can add cooked shredded chicken to the soup along with the rice.
- Serve Avgolemono soup hot as a comforting starter or light meal, accompanied by crusty bread or a Greek salad.

This soup is not only delicious but also comforting and perfect for any time of year. Its unique combination of flavors makes it a favorite in Greek cuisine. Enjoy your homemade Avgolemono soup!

Koulourakia (Greek Butter Cookies)

Ingredients:

- 1 cup unsalted butter, softened
- 1 cup granulated sugar
- 2 eggs
- 1/2 cup milk
- 1 tsp vanilla extract
- 4 cups all-purpose flour
- 2 tsp baking powder
- 1/4 tsp salt
- 1 egg yolk mixed with 1 tbsp milk, for egg wash
- Sesame seeds or almond slices, for topping (optional)

Instructions:

1. **Preheat Oven and Prepare Baking Sheets:**
   - Preheat your oven to 350°F (175°C). Line baking sheets with parchment paper or silicone baking mats.
2. **Cream Butter and Sugar:**
   - In a large bowl, cream together the softened butter and granulated sugar until light and fluffy.
3. **Add Eggs and Flavorings:**
   - Add the eggs one at a time, beating well after each addition. Mix in the milk and vanilla extract until well combined.
4. **Mix Dry Ingredients:**
   - In a separate bowl, whisk together the flour, baking powder, and salt.
5. **Combine Wet and Dry Ingredients:**
   - Gradually add the dry ingredients to the wet ingredients, mixing until a soft dough forms. The dough should be smooth and slightly sticky.
6. **Shape the Cookies:**
   - Pinch off pieces of dough and roll them into ropes about 4-5 inches long and 1/2 inch thick. Shape the ropes into twists, knots, or braids, or any desired shape.
   - Place the shaped cookies on the prepared baking sheets, spacing them about 1 inch apart.
7. **Brush with Egg Wash and Add Toppings:**
   - In a small bowl, mix together the egg yolk and 1 tbsp of milk to create an egg wash. Brush the tops of the cookies with the egg wash.
   - Sprinkle sesame seeds or press almond slices gently onto the tops of the cookies, if desired.
8. **Bake the Cookies:**
   - Bake in the preheated oven for 12-15 minutes, or until the cookies are lightly golden brown around the edges.

9. **Cool and Store:**
    - Remove the cookies from the oven and let them cool on the baking sheets for a few minutes. Transfer to a wire rack to cool completely.
    - Store koulourakia in an airtight container at room temperature. They will keep well for several days.

Notes:

- Koulourakia can be customized with different shapes and toppings according to your preference or the occasion.
- These cookies are perfect for serving with coffee or tea, or as a sweet treat during festive gatherings or celebrations.

Enjoy these delicious Greek butter cookies with their rich buttery taste and delicate texture!

Galaktoboureko (Custard Pastry)

Ingredients:

For the Custard Filling:

- 4 cups whole milk
- 1 cup fine semolina flour
- 1 cup granulated sugar
- 4 large eggs
- 1 tsp vanilla extract
- Zest of 1 lemon
- 1/2 cup unsalted butter, softened

For the Phyllo Layers:

- 1 package (16 oz) phyllo dough, thawed according to package instructions
- 1 cup unsalted butter, melted

For the Syrup:

- 2 cups water
- 2 cups granulated sugar
- Juice of 1/2 lemon

Instructions:

1. **Prepare the Custard Filling:**
   - In a saucepan, heat the milk over medium heat until it just begins to simmer. Remove from heat.
   - In a large bowl, whisk together the semolina flour, sugar, eggs, vanilla extract, and lemon zest until smooth.
   - Gradually pour the hot milk into the semolina mixture, whisking constantly to combine.
   - Return the mixture to the saucepan and cook over medium heat, stirring constantly, until thickened to a custard consistency, about 5-7 minutes.
   - Remove from heat and stir in the softened butter until well incorporated. Set aside to cool slightly.
2. **Assemble the Galaktoboureko:**
   - Preheat your oven to 350°F (175°C). Butter a 9x13 inch baking dish.
   - Unroll the phyllo dough and cover it with a damp towel to keep it from drying out.
   - Place one sheet of phyllo dough in the baking dish and brush lightly with melted butter. Repeat this process, layering about 10 sheets of phyllo dough, brushing each layer with butter.
3. **Add the Custard Filling:**

- Spread the prepared custard filling evenly over the top layer of phyllo dough.
4. **Layer the Remaining Phyllo Dough:**
    - Continue layering the remaining phyllo sheets on top of the custard filling, brushing each sheet with melted butter. Make sure to brush the top layer generously with butter.
5. **Bake the Galaktoboureko:**
    - Using a sharp knife, score the top layers of phyllo into diamond or square shapes, being careful not to cut through the bottom layers.
    - Bake in the preheated oven for 45-50 minutes, or until the top is golden brown and crispy.
6. **Prepare the Syrup:**
    - While the Galaktoboureko is baking, prepare the syrup. In a saucepan, combine the water, sugar, and lemon juice. Bring to a boil over medium-high heat, stirring occasionally.
    - Reduce heat and simmer for 10-15 minutes, until slightly thickened into a syrup consistency.
7. **Pour Syrup Over the Pastry:**
    - Once the Galaktoboureko is done baking and while it is still hot out of the oven, carefully pour the hot syrup evenly over the pastry. Allow it to soak and cool completely in the baking dish.
8. **Serve:**
    - Once cooled, cut through the pre-cut lines all the way to the bottom again and serve at room temperature.

Galaktoboureko is best served at room temperature, allowing the flavors to meld together. It's a deliciously sweet and creamy dessert that showcases the delicate layers of phyllo and rich custard filling. Enjoy this wonderful taste of Greek cuisine!

Loukoumades (Greek Honey Puffs)

Ingredients:

For the Dough:

- 1 packet (2 1/4 tsp) active dry yeast
- 1 1/2 cups warm water (about 110°F or 45°C)
- 3 1/2 cups all-purpose flour
- 1/2 tsp salt
- Vegetable oil, for frying

For the Honey Syrup:

- 1 cup honey
- 1/2 cup water
- 1 cinnamon stick (optional)
- Zest of 1 lemon (optional)

For Serving:

- Ground cinnamon (optional)
- Chopped walnuts or sesame seeds (optional)

Instructions:

1. **Prepare the Dough:**
   - In a small bowl, dissolve the yeast in the warm water. Let it sit for about 5-10 minutes until frothy.
2. **Mix the Dough:**
   - In a large mixing bowl, combine the flour and salt. Make a well in the center and pour in the yeast mixture. Stir until well combined and a sticky dough forms.
3. **Let the Dough Rise:**
   - Cover the bowl with a clean kitchen towel and let the dough rise in a warm place for about 1-2 hours, or until doubled in size.
4. **Make the Honey Syrup:**
   - While the dough is rising, prepare the honey syrup. In a saucepan, combine the honey, water, cinnamon stick (if using), and lemon zest (if using). Bring to a boil over medium heat, then reduce heat and simmer for about 5 minutes. Remove from heat and set aside to cool slightly.
5. **Heat the Oil:**
   - In a deep pot or fryer, heat vegetable oil to 350°F (175°C) over medium heat.
6. **Shape and Fry the Loukoumades:**

- Once the dough has risen, lightly oil your hands and pinch off pieces of dough (about the size of a walnut) and shape into rounds or small balls. You can also use two spoons to drop the dough into the hot oil.

7. **Fry Until Golden Brown:**
   - Carefully drop a few pieces of dough into the hot oil, being careful not to overcrowd the pot. Fry until golden brown and crispy, turning occasionally with a slotted spoon, about 2-3 minutes per batch.

8. **Drain and Soak:**
   - Remove the loukoumades from the oil using a slotted spoon and drain on paper towels briefly.
   - Immediately dip the hot loukoumades into the warm honey syrup, coating them evenly.

9. **Serve:**
   - Arrange the loukoumades on a serving platter. Sprinkle with ground cinnamon, chopped walnuts, or sesame seeds if desired.
   - Serve warm and enjoy these delicious Greek honey puffs as a delightful dessert or sweet treat!

Loukoumades are best enjoyed fresh and warm, soaking up the honey syrup for a sweet and satisfying bite. They are perfect for sharing with family and friends on special occasions or during festive gatherings.

Tiropita (Cheese Pie)

Ingredients:

For the Cheese Filling:

- 1 lb feta cheese, crumbled
- 1/2 lb ricotta cheese
- 1/2 lb Greek yogurt (or substitute with cottage cheese)
- 2 eggs
- 1/4 cup finely chopped fresh parsley
- 1/4 cup finely chopped fresh dill (optional)
- Freshly ground black pepper, to taste

For the Phyllo Dough and Assembly:

- 1 package (16 oz) phyllo dough, thawed according to package instructions
- 1 cup unsalted butter, melted
- Olive oil, for brushing the phyllo layers

Instructions:

1. **Prepare the Cheese Filling:**
   - In a large mixing bowl, combine the crumbled feta cheese, ricotta cheese, Greek yogurt, eggs, chopped parsley, chopped dill (if using), and black pepper. Mix well until all ingredients are evenly incorporated. Set aside.
2. **Prepare the Phyllo Dough:**
   - Preheat your oven to 350°F (175°C). Grease a 9x13 inch baking dish with olive oil or butter.
   - Unroll the phyllo dough sheets on a clean surface and cover with a damp towel to keep them from drying out.
3. **Assemble the Tiropita:**
   - Place one sheet of phyllo dough in the greased baking dish and brush lightly with melted butter. Repeat this process, layering about 8-10 sheets of phyllo dough, brushing each layer with melted butter.
   - Spread half of the cheese filling evenly over the phyllo layers.
4. **Continue Layering:**
   - Add another layer of 8-10 sheets of phyllo dough on top of the cheese filling, brushing each layer with melted butter.
   - Spread the remaining cheese filling evenly over the second layer of phyllo dough.
5. **Finish with Phyllo Layers:**
   - Add a final layer of 8-10 sheets of phyllo dough on top, brushing each layer with melted butter. Tuck any excess phyllo dough around the edges into the baking dish.
6. **Score and Bake:**

- Using a sharp knife, score the top layer of phyllo dough into diamond or square shapes, being careful not to cut through to the filling completely.
- Bake in the preheated oven for 45-50 minutes, or until the tiropita is golden brown and crispy on top.

7. **Serve:**
    - Remove from the oven and let it cool for a few minutes before slicing along the scored lines.
    - Serve warm or at room temperature as an appetizer or side dish. Tiropita pairs well with a fresh Greek salad or as part of a meze spread.

Tips:

- You can customize the cheese filling by adding other herbs such as mint or basil, or by adjusting the amount of pepper to suit your taste.
- Leftover tiropita can be stored in an airtight container in the refrigerator for a few days. Reheat in the oven or toaster oven to maintain its crispiness.

Enjoy this delicious Tiropita, with its layers of flaky phyllo and creamy cheese filling, as a taste of authentic Greek cuisine!

Revani (Semolina Cake)

Ingredients:

For the Cake:

- 1 cup fine semolina flour
- 1 cup all-purpose flour
- 1 cup granulated sugar
- 1 cup plain Greek yogurt
- 1/2 cup vegetable oil
- 1/2 cup fresh orange juice
- Zest of 1 orange
- 2 tsp baking powder
- 1/2 tsp baking soda
- 1/4 tsp salt
- 1/2 tsp vanilla extract

For the Syrup:

- 1 1/2 cups granulated sugar
- 1 1/2 cups water
- Juice of 1 lemon
- Zest of 1 lemon (optional)
- 1 cinnamon stick (optional)

Instructions:

1. **Prepare the Syrup:**
    - In a saucepan, combine the granulated sugar, water, lemon juice, lemon zest (if using), and cinnamon stick (if using). Bring to a boil over medium heat, stirring occasionally.
    - Reduce heat and simmer for 10-15 minutes, until the syrup slightly thickens. Remove from heat and set aside to cool.
2. **Make the Cake:**
    - Preheat your oven to 350°F (175°C). Grease a 9x13 inch baking dish with butter or oil.
    - In a large mixing bowl, whisk together the semolina flour, all-purpose flour, baking powder, baking soda, and salt.
3. **Prepare the Batter:**
    - In another bowl, whisk together the granulated sugar, Greek yogurt, vegetable oil, orange juice, orange zest, and vanilla extract until smooth and well combined.
    - Gradually add the dry ingredients to the wet ingredients, stirring until a smooth batter forms. Mix until just combined; do not overmix.
4. **Bake the Cake:**

- Pour the batter into the prepared baking dish and spread it evenly using a spatula.
- Bake in the preheated oven for 30-35 minutes, or until the top is golden brown and a toothpick inserted into the center comes out clean.

5. **Soak the Cake:**
    - While the cake is still hot from the oven, carefully pour the cooled syrup evenly over the top. Allow the syrup to soak into the cake completely.
6. **Cool and Serve:**
    - Let the Revani cool completely in the baking dish. Once cooled, cut into diamond-shaped pieces or squares.
    - Serve the Revani at room temperature. Optionally, garnish with chopped nuts like almonds or pistachios for added texture and flavor.

Tips:

- Ensure the syrup is cool while the cake is hot to allow for optimal absorption.
- Revani can be stored in an airtight container at room temperature for a few days. The flavors often improve as it sits.

Enjoy this delightful Greek dessert, Revani, with its tender crumb and aromatic syrup—a perfect treat for any occasion!

Stifado (Greek Beef Stew)

Ingredients:

- 2 lbs beef stew meat, cut into cubes
- 4-5 large onions, thinly sliced
- 4 cloves garlic, minced
- 2 tbsp olive oil
- 2 tbsp tomato paste
- 1/2 cup red wine (optional)
- 1/2 cup beef broth or water
- 1 tbsp red wine vinegar (or balsamic vinegar)
- 2 bay leaves
- 1 cinnamon stick
- 1 tsp dried oregano
- 1/2 tsp ground cloves
- 1/2 tsp ground allspice
- Salt and pepper, to taste
- Fresh parsley, chopped (for garnish, optional)

Instructions:

1. **Prepare the Beef:**
   - Pat the beef cubes dry with paper towels and season generously with salt and pepper.
2. **Sauté Onions and Garlic:**
   - In a large Dutch oven or heavy-bottomed pot, heat the olive oil over medium-high heat. Add the sliced onions and cook, stirring frequently, until softened and caramelized, about 10-12 minutes.
   - Add the minced garlic and cook for another 1-2 minutes until fragrant.
3. **Brown the Beef:**
   - Push the onions and garlic to the sides of the pot and add the seasoned beef cubes in batches. Brown the beef on all sides, about 5-7 minutes per batch. This step adds flavor to the stew.
4. **Add Tomato Paste and Deglaze:**
   - Stir in the tomato paste and cook for 1-2 minutes to caramelize slightly.
   - If using red wine, pour it into the pot and stir, scraping up any browned bits from the bottom of the pot.
5. **Add Remaining Ingredients:**
   - Pour in the beef broth (or water) and red wine vinegar. Add the bay leaves, cinnamon stick, dried oregano, ground cloves, and ground allspice. Stir to combine.
6. **Simmer the Stew:**

- Bring the stew to a boil, then reduce the heat to low. Cover the pot and simmer gently for 1.5 to 2 hours, or until the beef is tender and the flavors have melded together. Stir occasionally and add more broth or water if needed to maintain the desired consistency.
7. **Serve:**
    - Once the beef is tender and the stew has thickened, taste and adjust seasoning with salt and pepper if necessary.
    - Remove the bay leaves and cinnamon stick before serving.
    - Garnish with chopped fresh parsley if desired.
8. **Serve with Accompaniments:**
    - Stifado is traditionally served hot, often with rice, orzo pasta, or crusty bread to soak up the delicious sauce.

Tips:

- Stifado can be made ahead of time and tastes even better the next day as the flavors continue to develop.
- You can customize the stew by adding potatoes, carrots, or other vegetables if desired.

Enjoy this comforting and aromatic Greek beef stew, Stifado, which showcases the rich flavors of Mediterranean cuisine!

Melitzanosalata (Eggplant Dip)

Ingredients:

- 2 large eggplants
- 2-3 cloves garlic, minced
- 1/4 cup extra virgin olive oil, plus extra for drizzling
- 1-2 tbsp fresh lemon juice (adjust to taste)
- 2 tbsp chopped fresh parsley, plus extra for garnish
- Salt and pepper, to taste
- Optional: chopped tomatoes, red onion, or crumbled feta cheese for garnish

Instructions:

1. **Prepare the Eggplants:**
   - Preheat the oven to 400°F (200°C). Prick the eggplants with a fork in several places and place them on a baking sheet lined with parchment paper.
   - Roast the eggplants in the oven for about 45-60 minutes, turning occasionally, until the skins are charred and the flesh is soft and collapsed. Alternatively, you can grill the eggplants over an open flame until charred and tender.
2. **Peel and Drain:**
   - Remove the eggplants from the oven and let them cool slightly until they are safe to handle. Peel off the charred skins and discard. Place the flesh in a colander to drain excess liquid for about 15-20 minutes.
3. **Prepare the Dip:**
   - In a food processor or blender, combine the drained eggplant flesh, minced garlic, olive oil, and lemon juice. Blend until smooth and creamy. You can also mash the eggplant with a fork for a chunkier texture if desired.
4. **Season and Garnish:**
   - Stir in the chopped parsley and season with salt and pepper to taste. Adjust lemon juice and olive oil according to your preference for acidity and richness.
5. **Chill and Serve:**
   - Transfer the Melitzanosalata to a serving bowl. Drizzle with extra olive oil and garnish with additional chopped parsley, chopped tomatoes, red onion, or crumbled feta cheese if desired.
   - Refrigerate for at least 1 hour before serving to allow the flavors to meld together.
6. **Serve:**
   - Serve Melitzanosalata chilled or at room temperature as a dip with pita bread, crusty bread, or as a spread on sandwiches. It's also delicious served alongside grilled meats or vegetables.

Tips:

- You can adjust the garlic and lemon juice to suit your taste preferences.

- For a smokier flavor, you can char the eggplants directly over an open flame or grill them instead of roasting in the oven.
- Melitzanosalata can be stored in an airtight container in the refrigerator for up to 3-4 days.

Enjoy this creamy and flavorful Greek eggplant dip, Melitzanosalata, as a delicious addition to your Mediterranean-inspired meals!

Gyro Sandwich

Ingredients:

For the Gyro Meat:

- 1 lb lamb, beef, or a combination (thinly sliced, or ground meat)
- 2 cloves garlic, minced
- 1 tsp dried oregano
- 1 tsp dried thyme
- 1 tsp paprika
- 1/2 tsp ground cumin
- 1/2 tsp ground coriander
- Salt and pepper, to taste
- Olive oil, for cooking

For Serving:

- Pita bread or flatbread
- Tzatziki sauce (recipe below)
- Sliced tomatoes
- Sliced red onions
- Chopped fresh parsley or cilantro
- Optional: sliced cucumbers, shredded lettuce, crumbled feta cheese

Instructions:

1. **Prepare the Gyro Meat:**
    - If using thinly sliced meat: In a bowl, combine the sliced meat with minced garlic, dried oregano, thyme, paprika, cumin, coriander, salt, pepper, and a drizzle of olive oil. Toss to coat evenly and let it marinate for at least 30 minutes.
    - If using ground meat: Mix the ground meat with minced garlic, dried oregano, thyme, paprika, cumin, coriander, salt, pepper, and form into small patties or logs.
2. **Cook the Gyro Meat:**
    - Heat a grill pan or skillet over medium-high heat. Cook the marinated sliced meat for a few minutes on each side until cooked through and nicely browned. If using ground meat, cook the patties or logs until fully cooked through and browned on all sides.
3. **Prepare Tzatziki Sauce:**
    - In a bowl, combine 1 cup Greek yogurt, 1/2 cucumber (grated and excess liquid squeezed out), 1-2 cloves minced garlic, 1 tbsp olive oil, 1 tbsp lemon juice, 1 tbsp chopped fresh dill (or mint), salt, and pepper to taste. Mix well and refrigerate until ready to use.
4. **Assemble the Gyro Sandwich:**

- Warm the pita bread or flatbread. Spread a generous amount of Tzatziki sauce on the bread.
- Arrange the cooked gyro meat on top of the sauce.
- Add sliced tomatoes, sliced red onions, chopped parsley or cilantro, and any optional toppings like cucumbers, lettuce, or crumbled feta cheese.

5. **Serve:**
    - Fold the pita bread or flatbread around the gyro meat and toppings to form a sandwich.
    - Serve immediately and enjoy your homemade Gyro sandwich!

Tips:

- You can adjust the seasoning and spices according to your taste preferences.
- If you don't have a grill pan or skillet, you can also cook the meat on an outdoor grill or even bake it in the oven.
- For an authentic touch, consider adding a sprinkle of dried oregano or a squeeze of lemon juice over the assembled sandwich.

Enjoy this flavorful and satisfying Gyro sandwich, packed with Mediterranean flavors and textures!

Kleftiko (Greek Lamb)

Ingredients:

- 2 lbs lamb shoulder or leg, bone-in, cut into large chunks
- 4-5 cloves garlic, minced
- Juice of 1-2 lemons (about 1/4 cup)
- Zest of 1 lemon
- 1/4 cup extra virgin olive oil
- 1/2 cup dry white wine
- 1 tsp dried oregano
- 1 tsp dried thyme
- 1 tsp dried rosemary
- Salt and freshly ground black pepper, to taste
- 1/2 cup water or chicken broth (optional, for added moisture)

Instructions:

1. **Marinate the Lamb:**
   - In a large bowl or resealable plastic bag, combine the lamb chunks with minced garlic, lemon juice, lemon zest, olive oil, white wine, dried oregano, dried thyme, dried rosemary, salt, and pepper. Mix well to coat the lamb evenly. Marinate in the refrigerator for at least 2 hours, preferably overnight for best flavor.
2. **Preheat the Oven:**
   - Preheat your oven to 325°F (160°C).
3. **Prepare the Cooking Vessel:**
   - Transfer the marinated lamb and all the marinade into a large Dutch oven or roasting pan. If desired, add 1/2 cup of water or chicken broth to the pan to create steam and keep the lamb moist during cooking.
4. **Slow Cook the Lamb:**
   - Cover the Dutch oven or roasting pan tightly with a lid or aluminum foil.
   - Place in the preheated oven and roast for about 3-4 hours, or until the lamb is tender and falls off the bone easily. Check occasionally during cooking and add more water or broth if needed to prevent the pan from drying out.
5. **Finish and Serve:**
   - Once the lamb is tender, remove from the oven. Carefully uncover the pan to allow any excess liquid to evaporate and the lamb to brown slightly on top.
   - Serve the Kleftiko hot, garnished with fresh herbs like parsley or oregano, and accompanied by traditional Greek sides such as roasted potatoes, rice, or a Greek salad.

Tips:

- For an even richer flavor, you can sear the marinated lamb chunks in a hot skillet with a bit of olive oil before transferring them to the Dutch oven or roasting pan.
- Kleftiko is traditionally cooked slowly at low temperatures to achieve tender, melt-in-your-mouth meat. Patience is key to allow the flavors to develop fully.
- Leftover Kleftiko can be stored in an airtight container in the refrigerator for a few days. It can also be frozen for longer storage.

Enjoy this classic Greek dish of Kleftiko, where the lamb becomes beautifully tender and infused with Mediterranean herbs and citrus flavors through slow roasting!

Gemista (Stuffed Vegetables)

Ingredients:

- 6-8 medium-sized vegetables (such as tomatoes, bell peppers, zucchini, or eggplants)
- 1 cup long-grain rice (such as Carolina or Basmati)
- 1 medium onion, finely chopped
- 2-3 cloves garlic, minced
- 1/2 cup chopped fresh parsley
- 1/4 cup chopped fresh dill (optional)
- 1/4 cup chopped fresh mint (optional)
- 1/2 cup tomato sauce or puree
- 1/4 cup extra virgin olive oil, plus extra for drizzling
- Juice of 1 lemon
- Salt and freshly ground black pepper, to taste
- 1 cup vegetable or chicken broth, or water
- Optional: 1/2 lb ground beef or lamb (if adding meat)

Instructions:

1. **Prepare the Vegetables:**
   - Preheat your oven to 375°F (190°C).
   - Wash the vegetables well. For tomatoes and bell peppers, cut off the tops and carefully hollow them out using a spoon, removing the seeds and pulp while keeping the walls intact. For zucchini and eggplants, cut them in half lengthwise and scoop out the flesh, leaving a shell about 1/4 inch thick. Set the hollowed-out vegetables aside.
2. **Prepare the Filling:**
   - In a large bowl, combine the rice, chopped onion, minced garlic, chopped parsley, chopped dill and mint (if using), tomato sauce or puree, olive oil, lemon juice, salt, and pepper. If adding meat, mix in the ground beef or lamb.
   - Mix everything well to combine thoroughly.
3. **Stuff the Vegetables:**
   - Stuff each hollowed-out vegetable with the rice mixture, packing it gently but firmly. Leave a little space at the top of each vegetable as the rice will expand during cooking.
   - Place the stuffed vegetables upright in a large baking dish or roasting pan. If there is any remaining filling, you can place it around the vegetables in the dish.
4. **Bake the Gemista:**
   - Pour the vegetable or chicken broth (or water) into the baking dish around the stuffed vegetables. Drizzle a bit of olive oil over each stuffed vegetable.
   - Cover the baking dish with aluminum foil and bake in the preheated oven for about 1 hour. After 1 hour, uncover the dish and bake for an additional 30-45 minutes, or until the vegetables are tender and the rice is fully cooked and fluffy.

5. **Serve:**
    - Remove from the oven and let the Gemista cool slightly before serving.
    - Serve warm or at room temperature, garnished with extra chopped herbs if desired.

Tips:

- You can customize the filling by adding pine nuts, raisins, or grated cheese to the rice mixture for additional flavor and texture.
- Gemista can be served as a main dish or as a side dish alongside Greek yogurt or a simple salad.
- Leftover Gemista can be stored in the refrigerator for a few days and reheated in the oven or microwave.

Enjoy this delicious and comforting Greek dish of Gemista, perfect for showcasing seasonal vegetables and Mediterranean flavors!

Saganaki (Fried Cheese)

Ingredients:

- 8 oz kefalotyri cheese or graviera cheese (or substitute with halloumi or feta)
- 1/4 cup all-purpose flour
- 1/4 cup olive oil
- 1 lemon, cut into wedges
- Optional garnish: chopped fresh parsley, dried oregano, or red pepper flakes

Instructions:

1. **Prepare the Cheese:**
   - If using kefalotyri or graviera cheese, cut it into slices about 1/2 inch thick. If using halloumi, cut it into slices about 1/4 inch thick. If using feta, cut it into blocks or thick slices.
2. **Coat the Cheese:**
   - Place the flour in a shallow dish or plate. Dredge each piece of cheese in the flour, shaking off any excess.
3. **Heat the Oil:**
   - In a large skillet or frying pan, heat the olive oil over medium-high heat until shimmering.
4. **Fry the Cheese:**
   - Carefully add the coated cheese slices to the hot oil. Fry each side until golden brown and crispy, about 1-2 minutes per side. Use a spatula to carefully flip the cheese slices to prevent them from breaking.
5. **Serve:**
   - Once all sides are golden and crispy, transfer the fried cheese to a serving plate.
   - Squeeze fresh lemon juice over the saganaki and garnish with chopped fresh parsley, dried oregano, or red pepper flakes if desired.
6. **Enjoy Immediately:**
   - Serve the saganaki hot, while the cheese is still gooey and melty inside. It's typically enjoyed as a starter or meze dish with crusty bread to mop up the delicious oil and cheese.

Tips:

- Saganaki is best served immediately after frying, as the cheese can become tough when reheated.
- Experiment with different cheeses to find your favorite variation. Each cheese will bring a unique flavor and texture to the dish.
- Be cautious when frying the cheese as it can splatter. Use a splatter guard if needed and flip the cheese gently to avoid breaking it apart.

Enjoy this delightful and indulgent Greek appetizer of saganaki, perfect for sharing and enjoying with friends and family!

Yemista (Stuffed Bell Peppers)

Ingredients:

- 6-8 medium bell peppers (red, yellow, or green)
- 1 cup long-grain rice (such as Carolina or Basmati)
- 1 medium onion, finely chopped
- 2-3 cloves garlic, minced
- 1/2 cup chopped fresh parsley
- 1/4 cup chopped fresh dill (optional)
- 1/4 cup chopped fresh mint (optional)
- 1/2 cup tomato sauce or puree
- 1/4 cup extra virgin olive oil, plus extra for drizzling
- Juice of 1 lemon
- Salt and freshly ground black pepper, to taste
- 1 cup vegetable or chicken broth, or water
- Optional: 1/2 lb ground beef or lamb (if adding meat)

Instructions:

1. **Prepare the Bell Peppers:**
    - Preheat your oven to 375°F (190°C).
    - Cut off the tops of the bell peppers and carefully remove the seeds and membranes. Rinse the peppers well under cold water and set them aside.
2. **Prepare the Filling:**
    - In a large bowl, combine the rice, chopped onion, minced garlic, chopped parsley, chopped dill and mint (if using), tomato sauce or puree, olive oil, lemon juice, salt, and pepper. If adding meat, mix in the ground beef or lamb.
    - Mix everything well to combine thoroughly.
3. **Stuff the Bell Peppers:**
    - Stuff each bell pepper with the rice mixture, packing it gently but firmly. Leave a little space at the top of each pepper as the rice will expand during cooking.
    - Place the stuffed bell peppers upright in a large baking dish or roasting pan. If there is any remaining filling, you can place it around the peppers in the dish.
4. **Bake the Yemista:**
    - Pour the vegetable or chicken broth (or water) into the baking dish around the stuffed bell peppers. Drizzle a bit of olive oil over each stuffed pepper.
    - Cover the baking dish with aluminum foil and bake in the preheated oven for about 1 hour. After 1 hour, uncover the dish and bake for an additional 30-45 minutes, or until the peppers are tender and the rice is fully cooked and fluffy.
5. **Serve:**
    - Remove from the oven and let the Yemista cool slightly before serving.
    - Serve warm or at room temperature, garnished with extra chopped herbs if desired.

Tips:

- You can customize the filling by adding pine nuts, raisins, or grated cheese to the rice mixture for additional flavor and texture.
- Yemista can be served as a main dish or as a side dish alongside Greek yogurt or a simple salad.
- Leftover Yemista can be stored in the refrigerator for a few days and reheated in the oven or microwave.

Enjoy this classic Greek dish of Yemista, showcasing the vibrant flavors of Mediterranean cuisine and the natural sweetness of bell peppers!

Greek Yogurt with Honey and Nuts

Ingredients:

- 1 cup Greek yogurt (plain, full-fat or low-fat, depending on preference)
- 2-3 tbsp honey (adjust to taste)
- 1/4 cup mixed nuts (such as walnuts, almonds, pistachios, or pecans), chopped
- Optional: fresh berries or sliced fruits for garnish

Instructions:

1. **Prepare the Yogurt:**
   - Spoon the Greek yogurt into a serving bowl or individual bowls.
2. **Drizzle with Honey:**
   - Drizzle honey evenly over the Greek yogurt. You can adjust the amount of honey based on your sweetness preference.
3. **Add Nuts:**
   - Sprinkle the chopped mixed nuts over the yogurt and honey mixture. You can lightly toast the nuts beforehand for extra flavor if desired.
4. **Garnish (Optional):**
   - If desired, garnish with fresh berries or sliced fruits on top for added freshness and color.
5. **Serve Immediately:**
   - Serve the Greek yogurt with honey and nuts immediately, allowing everyone to mix the honey and nuts into the yogurt just before eating to maintain the crunchiness of the nuts.

Tips:

- Greek yogurt is thick and creamy, making it a great base for this simple dessert or snack.
- The combination of creamy yogurt, sweet honey, and crunchy nuts provides a delightful contrast in textures and flavors.
- Feel free to customize the recipe by adding other toppings such as granola, dried fruits, or a sprinkle of cinnamon for extra flavor.

Enjoy this refreshing and nutritious Greek yogurt with honey and nuts as a satisfying and wholesome treat any time of the day!

Psarosoupa (Fish Soup)

Ingredients:

- 1 lb mixed fish fillets (such as cod, haddock, or snapper), cut into chunks
- 1 onion, finely chopped
- 2-3 garlic cloves, minced
- 2 carrots, diced
- 2 celery stalks, diced
- 1 large potato, peeled and diced
- 1/2 cup dry white wine
- 4 cups fish or vegetable broth
- 1 bay leaf
- 1 tsp dried oregano
- 1 tsp dried thyme
- 1/2 tsp paprika
- Salt and freshly ground black pepper, to taste
- Juice of 1 lemon
- Fresh parsley, chopped (for garnish)
- Extra virgin olive oil, for drizzling

Instructions:

1. **Prepare the Vegetables:**
   - In a large pot or Dutch oven, heat a drizzle of olive oil over medium heat. Add the chopped onion, minced garlic, diced carrots, and diced celery. Sauté for about 5-7 minutes, until the vegetables start to soften.
2. **Add the Potato and Spices:**
   - Add the diced potato to the pot along with the bay leaf, dried oregano, dried thyme, paprika, salt, and pepper. Stir to combine and cook for another 2-3 minutes.
3. **Deglaze with Wine:**
   - Pour in the dry white wine and let it simmer for a few minutes to allow the alcohol to cook off and the flavors to meld together.
4. **Add Broth and Simmer:**
   - Pour in the fish or vegetable broth, and bring the soup to a gentle boil. Reduce the heat to low, cover the pot, and let it simmer for about 15-20 minutes, or until the vegetables are tender.
5. **Add Fish and Lemon Juice:**
   - Carefully add the fish chunks to the simmering soup. Cook for another 5-7 minutes, or until the fish is cooked through and flakes easily with a fork.
   - Stir in the lemon juice and adjust the seasoning with salt and pepper to taste.
6. **Serve:**

- Ladle the Psarosoupa into bowls. Garnish with chopped fresh parsley and drizzle with a bit of extra virgin olive oil.
- Serve hot, accompanied by crusty bread or a side salad if desired.

Tips:

- You can use a variety of fish fillets depending on availability and personal preference. Make sure to choose fish that are firm and will hold up well in the soup.
- Feel free to add other vegetables such as tomatoes or spinach for additional flavor and nutrition.
- Psarosoupa is often served with a slice of lemon on the side, allowing each person to adjust the acidity to their taste.

Enjoy this comforting and flavorful Greek fish soup, Psarosoupa, which is perfect for warming up on a chilly day and showcasing the fresh flavors of Mediterranean cuisine!

Melomakarona (Honey Cookies)

Ingredients:

For the Cookies:

- 1 cup vegetable oil
- 1/2 cup sugar
- 1/2 cup orange juice
- Zest of 1 orange
- 1/4 cup brandy or cognac (optional)
- 4 cups all-purpose flour
- 1/2 tsp baking soda
- 1/2 tsp baking powder
- 1/2 tsp ground cinnamon
- 1/4 tsp ground cloves
- 1/4 tsp salt
- 1/2 cup finely chopped walnuts or almonds

For the Syrup:

- 1 cup honey
- 1 cup water
- 1 cup sugar
- Zest of 1 lemon
- 1 cinnamon stick
- Whole cloves (optional)

Instructions:

1. **Prepare the Dough:**
    - In a large mixing bowl, whisk together the vegetable oil and sugar until well combined.
    - Add the orange juice, orange zest, and brandy (if using). Mix well.
2. **Combine Dry Ingredients:**
    - In a separate bowl, sift together the flour, baking soda, baking powder, ground cinnamon, ground cloves, and salt.
3. **Mix the Dough:**
    - Gradually add the dry ingredients to the wet ingredients, mixing until a soft dough forms. Be careful not to overmix.
    - Fold in the finely chopped nuts until evenly distributed.
4. **Shape the Cookies:**
    - Take small portions of the dough and shape them into oval or round cookies, about 1.5 inches in size. Place them on a baking sheet lined with parchment paper, leaving a bit of space between each cookie.

5. **Bake the Cookies:**
    - Preheat your oven to 350°F (175°C).
    - Bake the cookies for 20-25 minutes, or until they are golden brown and cooked through. Remove from the oven and let them cool completely on a wire rack.
6. **Prepare the Syrup:**
    - While the cookies are baking, prepare the syrup. In a medium saucepan, combine the honey, water, sugar, lemon zest, cinnamon stick, and whole cloves (if using). Bring to a boil over medium-high heat, then reduce the heat and simmer for 5-7 minutes. Remove from heat and let it cool slightly.
7. **Soak the Cookies:**
    - Dip each cooled cookie into the warm syrup, turning to coat evenly. Allow the cookies to soak in the syrup for a few seconds, then remove them with a slotted spoon and place them on a serving platter or tray.
8. **Optional Toppings:**
    - While the cookies are still sticky from the syrup, you can sprinkle them with additional finely chopped nuts or cinnamon for decoration.
9. **Serve and Store:**
    - Allow the cookies to cool completely and absorb the syrup before serving. Melomakarona are best stored in an airtight container at room temperature. They can be enjoyed for several days and actually improve in flavor as they sit.

Tips:

- Melomakarona are traditionally made during Christmas time in Greece and are often shared with family and friends.
- The syrup gives these cookies their characteristic moist texture and sweet flavor. Ensure the syrup is warm when dipping the cookies to allow them to soak it up properly.
- Feel free to adjust the spices and sweetness according to your preference. Some recipes also use a combination of honey and sugar for the syrup.

Enjoy these delightful Greek Melomakarona cookies, perfect for holiday celebrations or any time you crave a sweet treat with a hint of Mediterranean flair!

Greek Chicken with Orzo

Ingredients:

- 4 boneless, skinless chicken breasts
- Salt and freshly ground black pepper, to taste
- 2 tbsp olive oil
- 1 onion, finely chopped
- 3 cloves garlic, minced
- 1 red bell pepper, diced
- 1 yellow bell pepper, diced
- 1 cup cherry tomatoes, halved
- 1 cup orzo pasta
- 2 cups chicken broth
- 1 tsp dried oregano
- 1 tsp dried thyme
- 1/2 tsp dried rosemary
- Juice of 1 lemon
- 1/2 cup crumbled feta cheese
- Fresh parsley or dill, chopped (for garnish)
- Lemon wedges (for serving)

Instructions:

1. **Prepare the Chicken:**
   - Season the chicken breasts with salt and pepper on both sides.
   - In a large skillet or frying pan, heat 1 tablespoon of olive oil over medium-high heat. Add the chicken breasts and cook for about 5-6 minutes on each side, or until they are browned and cooked through. Remove the chicken from the pan and set aside.
2. **Cook the Vegetables:**
   - In the same skillet, add the remaining tablespoon of olive oil if needed. Add the chopped onion and cook for 2-3 minutes until softened.
   - Add the minced garlic, diced red and yellow bell peppers, and cherry tomatoes. Cook for another 3-4 minutes until the vegetables start to soften.
3. **Add Orzo and Broth:**
   - Stir in the orzo pasta, dried oregano, dried thyme, and dried rosemary. Cook for 1-2 minutes, stirring constantly, until the orzo is lightly toasted.
   - Pour in the chicken broth and lemon juice. Bring to a boil, then reduce the heat to medium-low. Cover and simmer for about 10-12 minutes, or until the orzo is tender and most of the liquid is absorbed, stirring occasionally.
4. **Combine Chicken and Orzo:**
   - Return the cooked chicken breasts to the skillet, nestling them into the orzo and vegetables. Cover and simmer for an additional 2-3 minutes to heat through.

5. **Serve:**
    - Sprinkle crumbled feta cheese over the top of the dish.
    - Garnish with chopped fresh parsley or dill.
    - Serve hot, with lemon wedges on the side for squeezing over the chicken and orzo.

Tips:

- You can customize this dish by adding other vegetables such as spinach or artichoke hearts.
- Adjust the seasoning and herbs according to your taste preference. Fresh herbs can also be used instead of dried herbs for a more vibrant flavor.
- Make sure to use a skillet or frying pan that has a lid, as covering the dish helps to cook the orzo evenly and keep the chicken moist.

Enjoy this delicious and satisfying Greek Chicken with Orzo, perfect for a cozy dinner with Mediterranean flavors!

Karidopita (Walnut Cake)

Ingredients:

For the Cake:

- 1 cup walnuts, finely chopped
- 1 cup breadcrumbs (or finely ground stale bread)
- 1 cup granulated sugar
- 1 cup vegetable oil (or melted butter)
- 1 cup orange juice
- Zest of 1 orange
- 1 tsp ground cinnamon
- 1/2 tsp ground cloves
- 1/2 tsp ground nutmeg
- 1 tsp baking powder
- 1 tsp baking soda
- 2 cups all-purpose flour

For the Syrup:

- 1 cup water
- 1 cup granulated sugar
- 1 cinnamon stick
- Zest of 1 lemon
- Juice of 1/2 lemon
- 1/2 cup honey

Instructions:

1. **Prepare the Cake:**
    - Preheat your oven to 350°F (175°C). Grease a 9x13 inch baking dish or cake pan, and dust with flour or line with parchment paper.
    - In a large mixing bowl, combine the chopped walnuts, breadcrumbs, sugar, vegetable oil (or melted butter), orange juice, orange zest, ground cinnamon, ground cloves, and ground nutmeg. Mix well until everything is thoroughly combined.
    - In a separate bowl, sift together the baking powder, baking soda, and all-purpose flour.
    - Gradually add the dry ingredients to the wet ingredients, mixing until just combined. Be careful not to overmix.
2. **Bake the Cake:**
    - Pour the batter into the prepared baking dish or cake pan, spreading it out evenly.

- Bake in the preheated oven for 35-40 minutes, or until a toothpick inserted into the center comes out clean and the top is golden brown.

3. **Prepare the Syrup:**
   - While the cake is baking, prepare the syrup. In a saucepan, combine the water, sugar, cinnamon stick, lemon zest, lemon juice, and honey. Bring to a boil over medium-high heat, then reduce the heat and simmer for 10-15 minutes, stirring occasionally, until slightly thickened.

4. **Soak the Cake:**
   - Once the cake is baked and while it is still hot, carefully pour the warm syrup over the entire surface of the cake, allowing it to soak in. Use a spoon to evenly distribute the syrup if needed.

5. **Let the Cake Cool:**
   - Allow the Karidopita to cool completely in the baking dish or cake pan, allowing the flavors to meld together and the syrup to fully absorb.

6. **Serve:**
   - Cut the cooled Karidopita into squares or diamond-shaped pieces.
   - Serve each piece with a sprinkle of extra chopped walnuts on top, if desired.

Tips:

- The breadcrumbs or finely ground stale bread in the cake batter contribute to the texture and moisture of the Karidopita. If using stale bread, make sure it is finely ground to avoid large pieces in the cake.
- You can adjust the amount of syrup according to your preference. Some prefer a more lightly soaked cake, while others enjoy it very moist.
- Karidopita is traditionally served as a dessert or sweet treat during holidays and special occasions in Greece. It pairs beautifully with a cup of Greek coffee or tea.

Enjoy this classic Greek Walnut Cake, Karidopita, with its aromatic spices and rich syrup for a delightful taste of Greek cuisine!

Kalamata Olive Bread

Ingredients:

- 3 cups all-purpose flour
- 1 cup warm water (about 110°F or 45°C)
- 1 packet (2 1/4 tsp) active dry yeast
- 1 tsp sugar
- 1 tsp salt
- 2 tbsp olive oil
- 1 cup Kalamata olives, pitted and chopped
- 1/2 cup crumbled feta cheese (optional)
- 1 tbsp chopped fresh rosemary (optional)
- Additional olive oil for brushing

Instructions:

1. **Activate the Yeast:**
   - In a small bowl, combine the warm water, yeast, and sugar. Stir gently and let it sit for about 5-10 minutes until frothy and bubbly.
2. **Mix the Dough:**
   - In a large mixing bowl or the bowl of a stand mixer fitted with a dough hook, combine the flour and salt.
   - Make a well in the center of the flour mixture and pour in the activated yeast mixture and olive oil.
   - Mix everything together until a dough forms. If using a stand mixer, knead the dough on low speed for about 5-7 minutes until it becomes smooth and elastic. If kneading by hand, knead on a lightly floured surface for about 10 minutes.
3. **Add Olives and Optional Ingredients:**
   - Add the chopped Kalamata olives, crumbled feta cheese (if using), and chopped fresh rosemary (if using) to the dough. Knead or mix until the olives and optional ingredients are evenly distributed throughout the dough.
4. **First Rise:**
   - Place the dough in a lightly oiled bowl, turning once to coat the dough with oil. Cover the bowl with a clean kitchen towel or plastic wrap and let it rise in a warm, draft-free place for about 1-1.5 hours, or until doubled in size.
5. **Shape the Bread:**
   - Once the dough has doubled in size, punch it down gently to deflate it. Shape the dough into a round or oval loaf, and place it on a parchment paper-lined baking sheet.
6. **Second Rise:**
   - Cover the shaped loaf with a clean kitchen towel or plastic wrap and let it rise for another 30-45 minutes, until it puffs up slightly.
7. **Preheat the Oven:**

- Meanwhile, preheat your oven to 375°F (190°C).
8. **Bake the Bread:**
    - Just before baking, lightly brush the top of the loaf with olive oil. Optionally, you can sprinkle a little sea salt or additional chopped rosemary on top for extra flavor.
    - Bake in the preheated oven for 30-35 minutes, or until the bread is golden brown and sounds hollow when tapped on the bottom.
    - Transfer the bread to a wire rack to cool completely before slicing.
9. **Serve:**
    - Slice and serve the Kalamata Olive Bread warm or at room temperature. It's delicious on its own, with butter, or as a side to soups and salads.

Tips:

- Ensure the olives are well-drained and pitted before chopping and adding them to the dough.
- The addition of feta cheese and rosemary adds extra flavor to the bread, but you can omit them if preferred or adjust the quantities to your taste.
- This bread keeps well for a few days when stored in an airtight container or wrapped tightly in plastic wrap.

Enjoy this homemade Kalamata Olive Bread, filled with the Mediterranean flavors of olives and optionally enhanced with feta and rosemary, perfect for sharing with friends and family!

Kolokithopita (Zucchini Pie)

Ingredients:

For the Filling:

- 2-3 medium zucchini, grated (about 4 cups grated zucchini)
- 1 onion, finely chopped
- 2-3 cloves garlic, minced
- 1/2 cup fresh dill, chopped
- 1/2 cup fresh parsley, chopped
- 1/2 cup crumbled feta cheese
- 1/2 cup grated Parmesan cheese
- Salt and freshly ground black pepper, to taste
- Olive oil for cooking

For the Dough:

- 1 package (16 oz) phyllo dough, thawed according to package instructions
- 1/2 cup melted butter or olive oil (for brushing layers)

Instructions:

1. **Prepare the Filling:**
   - Grate the zucchini using a box grater or food processor. Place the grated zucchini in a colander and sprinkle with salt. Let it sit for about 10-15 minutes, then squeeze out excess moisture using your hands or a clean kitchen towel.
   - In a large skillet, heat a drizzle of olive oil over medium heat. Add the chopped onion and sauté for 3-4 minutes until softened. Add the minced garlic and cook for another minute until fragrant.
   - Add the grated zucchini to the skillet and cook for about 5-7 minutes, stirring occasionally, until the zucchini is tender and any remaining moisture has evaporated.
   - Remove the skillet from heat and let the zucchini mixture cool slightly.
2. **Prepare the Dough:**
   - Preheat your oven to 350°F (175°C). Grease a 9x13 inch baking dish or a round baking pan.
   - Lay out the phyllo dough sheets on a clean, dry surface. Cover them with a damp kitchen towel to keep them from drying out as you work.
3. **Assemble the Pie:**
   - Brush a sheet of phyllo dough with melted butter or olive oil and place it into the baking dish, letting the edges hang over the sides. Repeat with 5-6 more sheets, brushing each layer with butter or oil.
   - Spread half of the zucchini mixture evenly over the phyllo dough.
   - Sprinkle half of the chopped dill and parsley over the zucchini mixture.

- Sprinkle half of the crumbled feta and grated Parmesan cheese over the herbs.
- Repeat the layering process with the remaining phyllo sheets (brushing each with butter or oil), zucchini mixture, herbs, and cheeses.

4. **Finish the Pie:**
   - Fold the overhanging phyllo edges over the top of the pie to create a rustic crust. Brush the top layer generously with melted butter or olive oil.
5. **Bake the Pie:**
   - Place the assembled kolokithopita in the preheated oven and bake for 35-40 minutes, or until the top is golden brown and crisp.
6. **Serve:**
   - Remove the pie from the oven and let it cool for a few minutes before slicing.
   - Serve warm or at room temperature. It pairs well with a fresh Greek salad or as part of a mezze spread.

Tips:

- You can customize the filling by adding other ingredients such as chopped spinach, mint, or green onions.
- Make sure to drain excess moisture from the zucchini to prevent the pie from becoming soggy.
- Phyllo dough can be fragile, so handle it gently and work quickly to prevent it from drying out.

Enjoy this delicious and flavorful Greek Kolokithopita, showcasing the wonderful taste of zucchini and Mediterranean herbs!

Pasteli (Sesame Seed and Honey Bars)

Ingredients:

- 1 cup sesame seeds
- 1/2 cup honey (preferably Greek thyme honey)

Instructions:

1. **Toast the Sesame Seeds:**
    - In a dry skillet or frying pan, toast the sesame seeds over medium heat. Stir frequently to ensure even toasting, and toast until they become fragrant and lightly golden brown. This should take about 5-7 minutes. Be careful not to burn them.
2. **Prepare the Honey:**
    - While the sesame seeds are toasting, warm the honey in a small saucepan over low heat. Warm it just enough to make it easier to mix with the sesame seeds, but do not let it boil.
3. **Combine Sesame Seeds and Honey:**
    - Once the sesame seeds are toasted, remove them from the heat and immediately pour them into a mixing bowl.
    - Pour the warm honey over the toasted sesame seeds. Stir quickly and thoroughly to coat all the sesame seeds evenly with honey.
4. **Shape the Pasteli:**
    - While the mixture is still warm and pliable, quickly transfer it onto a piece of parchment paper or a silicone mat.
    - Use a spatula or the back of a spoon to press the mixture evenly into a square or rectangular shape, about 1/4 to 1/2 inch thick.
5. **Let it Set:**
    - Allow the Pasteli to cool and set at room temperature for at least 1-2 hours, or until firm.
6. **Cut and Serve:**
    - Once the Pasteli is completely cooled and firm, use a sharp knife to cut it into small bars or squares.
    - Store the Pasteli in an airtight container at room temperature. It will keep well for several weeks, although it's so delicious it likely won't last that long!

Tips:

- Use high-quality sesame seeds for the best flavor. You can use white or black sesame seeds, or a combination of both.
- Greek thyme honey is traditionally used for its distinct flavor, but you can use any type of honey you prefer.

- If you want to add a twist, you can also mix in other ingredients such as nuts (like almonds or pistachios) or dried fruits (like chopped figs or apricots) before shaping the Pasteli.

Enjoy these homemade Pasteli bars as a nutritious snack or a sweet treat, perfect for sharing the flavors of Greece with friends and family!

Pitarakia (Fried Dough Pastries)

Ingredients:

- 4 cups all-purpose flour
- 1/2 cup sugar
- 1/2 tsp baking powder
- 1/2 tsp salt
- 1/2 cup unsalted butter, melted
- 1/2 cup milk
- 1/2 cup ouzo (Greek anise-flavored liqueur), or brandy, or water (adjust based on preference)
- Zest of 1 lemon
- Vegetable oil for frying
- Powdered sugar for dusting

Instructions:

1. **Prepare the Dough:**
    - In a large mixing bowl, whisk together the flour, sugar, baking powder, and salt.
    - Add the melted butter, milk, ouzo (or brandy or water), and lemon zest to the dry ingredients. Mix well until the dough comes together. It should be soft and slightly sticky. If too dry, add a little more milk; if too wet, add a little more flour.
2. **Shape the Pitarakia:**
    - On a lightly floured surface, divide the dough into smaller portions. Roll each portion into a ball, then roll it out into a thin circle or rectangle (about 1/8 inch thick).
    - Cut the dough into strips about 1 inch wide and 4-5 inches long.
    - Take each strip and twist it into a spiral or twist shape, pressing the ends lightly to seal.
3. **Fry the Pitarakia:**
    - In a deep frying pan or pot, heat vegetable oil over medium-high heat until it reaches about 350°F (175°C).
    - Carefully place a few pitarakia into the hot oil, without overcrowding the pan. Fry in batches for 2-3 minutes on each side, or until they are golden brown and crispy.
    - Use a slotted spoon or tongs to transfer the fried pitarakia to a plate lined with paper towels to drain excess oil.
4. **Serve:**
    - Allow the pitarakia to cool slightly before dusting generously with powdered sugar.
    - Serve warm or at room temperature.

Tips:

- Pitarakia can be enjoyed plain or with a variety of toppings or dips, such as honey, chocolate sauce, or fruit preserves.
- The ouzo or brandy adds flavor to the dough, but you can substitute with water if preferred.
- Be cautious when frying to ensure the oil is hot enough to fry the pitarakia quickly and evenly, but not too hot to burn them.

Enjoy these delicious Greek fried dough pastries, Pitarakia, as a special treat with a cup of Greek coffee or tea, or share them with friends and family during festive gatherings!

Octopus in Red Wine

Ingredients:

- 1 large octopus (about 2-3 lbs), cleaned and thawed if frozen
- 1 onion, finely chopped
- 3-4 garlic cloves, minced
- 1 cup red wine (choose a dry red wine like Merlot or Cabernet Sauvignon)
- 1/2 cup water
- 2 tbsp tomato paste
- 2-3 tbsp olive oil
- 1 bay leaf
- 1 tsp dried oregano
- Salt and freshly ground black pepper, to taste
- Fresh parsley, chopped (for garnish)

Instructions:

1. **Prepare the Octopus:**
   - If using fresh octopus, clean it thoroughly, removing the beak and eyes. If using frozen octopus, ensure it is fully thawed according to package instructions.
2. **Cook the Octopus:**
   - In a large pot, bring water to a boil. Add the octopus and cook for about 30-40 minutes, or until tender. The octopus should be easily pierced with a fork. Cooking time can vary depending on the size and freshness of the octopus.
   - Once cooked, remove the octopus from the pot and let it cool slightly. Cut the octopus into bite-sized pieces.
3. **Prepare the Red Wine Sauce:**
   - In a large skillet or frying pan, heat olive oil over medium heat. Add the chopped onion and cook for 3-4 minutes until softened.
   - Add the minced garlic and cook for another minute until fragrant.
   - Stir in the red wine, water, tomato paste, bay leaf, and dried oregano. Season with salt and pepper to taste.
4. **Simmer the Octopus:**
   - Add the octopus pieces to the skillet with the red wine sauce. Stir gently to combine.
   - Bring the mixture to a boil, then reduce the heat to low. Cover and simmer for about 30-40 minutes, stirring occasionally, until the sauce has reduced and thickened slightly.
5. **Serve:**
   - Remove the bay leaf from the octopus dish.
   - Transfer the Octopus in Red Wine to a serving platter or individual plates.
   - Garnish with chopped fresh parsley before serving.

Tips:

- Octopus can be tough if not cooked properly. To ensure tenderness, you can also tenderize it by freezing and thawing it before cooking, or by gently pounding it before boiling.
- Adjust the cooking time based on the size and thickness of the octopus. It should be tender but not overcooked.
- Serve Octopus in Red Wine with crusty bread to soak up the delicious sauce, or over a bed of rice or mashed potatoes.

Enjoy this flavorful Greek dish of Octopus in Red Wine, perfect for a special dinner with Mediterranean flair!

Kadaifi (Shredded Phyllo Pastry)

Ingredients:

For the Kadaifi Dough:

- 1 package (16 oz) Kadaifi dough (shredded phyllo dough)
- 1 cup unsalted butter, melted

For the Nut Filling:

- 1 cup walnuts, chopped
- 1 cup almonds, chopped
- 1/2 cup sugar
- 1 tsp ground cinnamon
- 1/4 tsp ground cloves
- 1/4 tsp ground nutmeg
- Zest of 1 lemon
- Zest of 1 orange

For the Syrup:

- 1 1/2 cups granulated sugar
- 1 cup water
- Juice of 1/2 lemon
- 1 cinnamon stick
- 1 strip of orange peel

Instructions:

1. **Prepare the Nut Filling:**
   - In a bowl, combine the chopped walnuts, almonds, sugar, ground cinnamon, ground cloves, ground nutmeg, lemon zest, and orange zest. Mix well and set aside.
2. **Prepare the Syrup:**
   - In a saucepan, combine the granulated sugar, water, lemon juice, cinnamon stick, and orange peel.
   - Bring the mixture to a boil over medium-high heat, stirring occasionally. Reduce the heat to low and simmer for about 10-15 minutes, until the syrup slightly thickens. Remove from heat and let it cool. Discard the cinnamon stick and orange peel.
3. **Assemble the Kadaifi:**
   - Preheat your oven to 350°F (175°C).
   - Separate the shredded phyllo dough strands gently with your fingers, loosening them up.

- Take a handful of the shredded phyllo dough and spread it out flat on a clean surface.
- Brush the dough with melted butter.
- Place a spoonful of the nut filling along one edge of the dough.
- Roll the dough tightly around the nut filling, like a cigar or jelly roll, tucking in the edges as you roll.
- Repeat with the remaining dough and nut filling.

4. **Bake the Kadaifi:**
   - Place the rolled Kadaifi pastries on a baking sheet lined with parchment paper, seam side down.
   - Bake in the preheated oven for 30-35 minutes, or until golden brown and crispy.

5. **Soak in Syrup:**
   - Remove the baked Kadaifi from the oven and immediately pour the cooled syrup evenly over the hot pastries. Allow the Kadaifi to absorb the syrup for at least 1 hour before serving.

6. **Serve:**
   - Serve Kadaifi warm or at room temperature.
   - Optionally, garnish with chopped nuts or a sprinkle of powdered sugar before serving.

Tips:

- Handle the shredded phyllo dough gently to prevent it from clumping together.
- Ensure the syrup is cooled slightly before pouring over the hot Kadaifi to allow for better absorption.
- Kadaifi pastries can be stored in an airtight container at room temperature for a few days. They may soften slightly over time but will still be delicious.

Enjoy this delightful Greek dessert of Kadaifi, with its crispy layers and nutty filling soaked in sweet syrup, perfect for special occasions and gatherings!

Keftedakia (Greek Meatballs)

Ingredients:

- 1 lb ground beef (you can also use a combination of beef and pork, or lamb)
- 1 small onion, finely chopped
- 2-3 garlic cloves, minced
- 1/2 cup breadcrumbs
- 1/4 cup milk
- 1 egg, lightly beaten
- 2 tbsp fresh parsley, finely chopped
- 1 tbsp fresh mint, finely chopped (optional)
- 1 tsp dried oregano
- 1/2 tsp ground cumin
- 1/4 tsp ground cinnamon
- Salt and freshly ground black pepper, to taste
- Olive oil, for frying

Instructions:

1. **Prepare the Breadcrumbs:**
   - In a small bowl, combine the breadcrumbs and milk. Let them soak for a few minutes until the breadcrumbs absorb the milk.
2. **Mix the Meatball Mixture:**
   - In a large mixing bowl, combine the ground beef, finely chopped onion, minced garlic, soaked breadcrumbs, beaten egg, chopped parsley, chopped mint (if using), dried oregano, ground cumin, ground cinnamon, salt, and pepper.
   - Use your hands or a spoon to mix everything together until well combined. Be careful not to overmix, as this can make the meatballs tough.
3. **Shape the Meatballs:**
   - Take small portions of the meat mixture and roll them between your palms to form meatballs, about 1-1.5 inches in diameter. Place the shaped meatballs on a plate or baking sheet lined with parchment paper.
4. **Cook the Meatballs:**
   - In a large skillet or frying pan, heat enough olive oil to coat the bottom of the pan over medium heat.
   - Once the oil is hot, add the meatballs in batches, making sure not to overcrowd the pan. Cook the meatballs for about 4-5 minutes on each side, or until they are browned and cooked through. Use tongs to turn them gently to avoid breaking them.
   - Remove the cooked meatballs from the skillet and place them on a plate lined with paper towels to absorb any excess oil.
5. **Serve:**
   - Arrange the Keftedakia on a serving platter.

- Serve them warm as a main dish with a side of tzatziki sauce, Greek salad, and pita bread. They are also delicious as part of a meze spread with other Greek appetizers.

Tips:

- You can adjust the seasoning and herbs according to your taste preferences. Some variations include adding more garlic, or using different herbs like dill or basil.
- If you prefer, you can bake the meatballs in the oven instead of frying them. Preheat the oven to 400°F (200°C), place the meatballs on a baking sheet lined with parchment paper, and bake for about 15-20 minutes, or until they are cooked through and golden brown.
- Keftedakia can be made ahead of time and reheated before serving. Store any leftovers in an airtight container in the refrigerator for up to 3 days.

Enjoy these flavorful and juicy Greek meatballs, Keftedakia, as a delicious main dish or appetizer!

Melitzanes Papoutsakia (Stuffed Eggplants)

Ingredients:

For the Eggplants:

- 4 medium-sized eggplants
- Olive oil, for brushing
- Salt and pepper, to taste

For the Meat Filling:

- 1 lb ground beef or lamb (or a combination)
- 1 onion, finely chopped
- 2-3 garlic cloves, minced
- 1/2 cup tomato sauce or passata
- 1/4 cup red wine (optional)
- 1 tsp dried oregano
- 1/2 tsp ground cinnamon
- Salt and pepper, to taste
- Olive oil, for cooking

For the Béchamel Sauce:

- 4 tbsp unsalted butter
- 1/4 cup all-purpose flour
- 2 cups milk, warmed
- Salt and pepper, to taste
- A pinch of ground nutmeg
- 1/2 cup grated Parmesan cheese (optional)

Additional Ingredients:

- Fresh parsley or dill, chopped (for garnish)
- Extra Parmesan cheese, for sprinkling (optional)

Instructions:

1. **Prepare the Eggplants:**
    - Preheat your oven to 400°F (200°C).
    - Wash the eggplants and cut them in half lengthwise. Score the flesh of each half with a sharp knife in a crisscross pattern, being careful not to cut through the skin.
    - Brush the cut sides of the eggplants with olive oil and season with salt and pepper. Place them on a baking sheet lined with parchment paper, cut side down.

- Roast the eggplants in the preheated oven for about 25-30 minutes, or until they are tender and lightly browned. Remove from the oven and set aside to cool slightly.

2. **Prepare the Meat Filling:**
   - While the eggplants are roasting, prepare the meat filling. In a large skillet or frying pan, heat a drizzle of olive oil over medium heat.
   - Add the chopped onion and cook for 3-4 minutes until softened and translucent. Add the minced garlic and cook for another minute until fragrant.
   - Add the ground beef or lamb to the skillet, breaking it up with a spoon. Cook until browned and cooked through.
   - Stir in the tomato sauce (or passata), red wine (if using), dried oregano, ground cinnamon, salt, and pepper. Simmer for 10-15 minutes until the flavors meld together and the sauce thickens slightly. Remove from heat and set aside.

3. **Prepare the Béchamel Sauce:**
   - In a medium saucepan, melt the butter over medium heat. Once melted, add the flour and whisk continuously for 1-2 minutes to cook the flour, but not letting it brown.
   - Gradually pour in the warmed milk, whisking constantly to avoid lumps. Cook the sauce until it thickens and coats the back of a spoon, about 5-7 minutes.
   - Season the béchamel sauce with salt, pepper, and a pinch of ground nutmeg. Stir in the grated Parmesan cheese (if using) until melted and smooth. Remove from heat and set aside.

4. **Assemble and Bake Melitzanes Papoutsakia:**
   - Reduce the oven temperature to 375°F (190°C).
   - Carefully scoop out the flesh of the roasted eggplants, leaving a thin shell. Chop the eggplant flesh and add it to the meat filling. Mix well.
   - Place the hollowed-out eggplant shells back on the baking sheet. Spoon the meat filling into each eggplant shell, dividing it evenly.
   - Top each stuffed eggplant with a generous amount of béchamel sauce, spreading it evenly to cover the meat filling.

5. **Bake:**
   - Bake the Melitzanes Papoutsakia in the preheated oven for 30-35 minutes, or until the béchamel sauce is golden brown and bubbly.

6. **Serve:**
   - Remove from the oven and let it cool for a few minutes before serving.
   - Garnish with chopped fresh parsley or dill, and optionally, sprinkle with extra Parmesan cheese.

Tips:

- You can customize the meat filling by adding chopped tomatoes, bell peppers, or even a splash of red wine for extra flavor.
- Melitzanes Papoutsakia can be made ahead of time and reheated before serving. Store any leftovers in an airtight container in the refrigerator for up to 3 days.

- Serve Melitzanes Papoutsakia as a main dish with a side of Greek salad and crusty bread for a complete meal.

Enjoy this comforting and flavorful Greek dish of Melitzanes Papoutsakia with its tender roasted eggplants, savory meat filling, and creamy béchamel sauce!

Bougatsa (Cream-Filled Pastry)

Ingredients:

For the Bougatsa:

- 1 package (16 oz) phyllo dough, thawed according to package instructions
- 1 cup unsalted butter, melted
- Powdered sugar and ground cinnamon, for dusting

For the Custard Filling:

- 4 cups whole milk
- 1 cup fine semolina flour (or use all-purpose flour if semolina is not available)
- 1 cup granulated sugar
- 1/4 tsp salt
- 2 tsp vanilla extract
- 4 large eggs
- Zest of 1 lemon
- Zest of 1 orange

Instructions:

1. **Prepare the Custard Filling:**
    - In a saucepan, heat the milk over medium heat until it just starts to simmer. Remove from heat.
    - In a large bowl, whisk together the semolina flour, sugar, and salt. Gradually add the hot milk to the semolina mixture, whisking constantly to prevent lumps.
    - Return the mixture to the saucepan and place it over medium-low heat. Cook, stirring constantly, until the mixture thickens and comes to a gentle boil. This should take about 5-7 minutes.
    - Remove from heat and stir in the vanilla extract, lemon zest, and orange zest. Let the custard mixture cool slightly.
    - In a separate bowl, lightly beat the eggs. Gradually add a small amount of the warm custard mixture to the eggs, whisking constantly, to temper the eggs. Then pour the egg mixture back into the saucepan with the remaining custard mixture, whisking constantly.
    - Return the saucepan to low heat and cook, stirring constantly, for another 2-3 minutes until the custard thickens further. Remove from heat and let it cool completely.
2. **Assemble the Bougatsa:**
    - Preheat your oven to 350°F (175°C). Grease a large baking dish (approximately 9x13 inches) with butter.

- Lay out one sheet of phyllo dough on a clean surface and brush it lightly with melted butter. Place another sheet of phyllo on top and brush with butter again. Repeat with 6-8 layers of phyllo dough, brushing each layer with melted butter.
- Spread the cooled custard filling evenly over the layered phyllo dough.
- Cover the custard with 6-8 more layers of phyllo dough, brushing each layer with melted butter as before.

3. **Bake the Bougatsa:**
   - Using a sharp knife, score the top layer of phyllo dough into diamond-shaped pieces or squares.
   - Bake in the preheated oven for 45-50 minutes, or until the phyllo is golden brown and crispy.

4. **Serve:**
   - Remove from the oven and let the Bougatsa cool slightly.
   - Dust generously with powdered sugar and ground cinnamon.
   - Cut into portions along the scored lines and serve warm.

Tips:

- Phyllo dough can dry out quickly, so keep it covered with a damp kitchen towel while you work with it.
- When assembling the Bougatsa, make sure to brush each layer of phyllo dough with melted butter to achieve that crispy texture.
- You can store leftover Bougatsa in the refrigerator. Reheat in the oven or microwave before serving.

Enjoy this classic Greek pastry, Bougatsa, with its creamy custard filling and crispy layers of phyllo dough, perfect for breakfast, brunch, or dessert!

Arni Lemonato (Lemon Garlic Lamb)

Ingredients:

- 1 leg of lamb or lamb shoulder, about 4-5 lbs, bone-in or boneless
- 6-8 garlic cloves, minced
- 1/2 cup olive oil
- 1 cup chicken or vegetable broth
- Juice of 2-3 lemons (about 1/2 to 3/4 cup)
- Zest of 1 lemon
- 2 tsp dried oregano
- 1 tsp dried thyme
- Salt and freshly ground black pepper, to taste
- Fresh parsley, chopped, for garnish

Instructions:

1. **Prepare the Lamb:**
   - Preheat your oven to 325°F (160°C).
   - If using a bone-in leg of lamb, trim excess fat and pat dry with paper towels. Season the lamb generously with salt and pepper.
2. **Marinate the Lamb:**
   - In a bowl, whisk together the minced garlic, olive oil, lemon juice, lemon zest, dried oregano, and dried thyme.
   - Place the lamb in a large roasting pan or baking dish. Pour the marinade over the lamb, turning to coat it evenly. Cover the dish with plastic wrap and let it marinate in the refrigerator for at least 2 hours, preferably overnight.
3. **Roast the Lamb:**
   - Remove the lamb from the refrigerator and let it come to room temperature for about 30 minutes before cooking.
   - Add the chicken or vegetable broth to the roasting pan.
   - Cover the roasting pan tightly with aluminum foil or a lid.
   - Roast in the preheated oven for about 3 to 3 1/2 hours, or until the lamb is tender and falling off the bone (if using bone-in).
   - Occasionally baste the lamb with the pan juices during cooking.
4. **Serve:**
   - Once cooked, remove the lamb from the oven and let it rest, covered loosely with foil, for about 15 minutes before carving.
   - Slice or shred the lamb and arrange it on a serving platter.
   - Spoon some of the pan juices over the lamb.
   - Garnish with chopped fresh parsley.
5. **Optional Sauce:**

- If desired, you can strain the pan juices into a saucepan and simmer over medium heat until slightly reduced. Adjust seasoning with salt and pepper if needed. Serve the sauce alongside the lamb.

Tips:

- For a more pronounced lemon flavor, you can increase the amount of lemon juice and zest according to your preference.
- Serve Arni Lemonato with traditional Greek sides like roasted potatoes, Greek salad, or steamed vegetables.
- Leftover lamb can be stored in an airtight container in the refrigerator for up to 3-4 days. Reheat gently in the oven or microwave before serving.

Enjoy this flavorful and comforting Greek dish of Arni Lemonato, showcasing tender lamb infused with lemon and garlic, perfect for a special dinner or festive gathering!

Loukoumades (Greek Donuts)

Ingredients:

For the Loukoumades:

- 1 package (2 1/4 tsp) active dry yeast
- 1 cup lukewarm water
- 1 tbsp granulated sugar
- 3 1/2 cups all-purpose flour
- 1/2 tsp salt
- Vegetable oil, for frying

For the Honey Syrup:

- 1 cup honey
- 1/2 cup water
- 1 cinnamon stick
- Zest of 1 lemon (optional)

For Serving:

- Ground cinnamon, for sprinkling
- Chopped nuts (such as walnuts or almonds), optional

Instructions:

1. **Prepare the Loukoumades Dough:**
   - In a small bowl, combine the lukewarm water, granulated sugar, and active dry yeast. Let it sit for about 5-10 minutes until frothy.
   - In a large mixing bowl, sift together the flour and salt.
   - Make a well in the center of the flour mixture and pour in the yeast mixture. Stir until well combined and a sticky dough forms.
   - Cover the bowl with a clean kitchen towel and let the dough rise in a warm, draft-free place for about 1-2 hours, or until it doubles in size.
2. **Make the Honey Syrup:**
   - In a saucepan, combine the honey, water, cinnamon stick, and lemon zest (if using). Bring to a boil over medium heat, stirring occasionally.
   - Reduce the heat to low and simmer for 5 minutes. Remove from heat and let it cool slightly. Discard the cinnamon stick and lemon zest.
3. **Fry the Loukoumades:**
   - In a deep frying pan or pot, heat vegetable oil to 350°F (175°C).
   - Using two spoons or a small ice cream scoop, drop spoonfuls of dough (about 1 tablespoon each) into the hot oil. You can also wet your hands and shape them into small balls before frying.

        - ○ Fry the loukoumades in batches, turning occasionally, until they are golden brown and cooked through, about 2-3 minutes per batch.
        - ○ Use a slotted spoon or spider strainer to remove the loukoumades from the oil and drain them on a plate lined with paper towels.
    4. **Serve the Loukoumades:**
        - ○ While still warm, drizzle the loukoumades with the honey syrup.
        - ○ Sprinkle with ground cinnamon and chopped nuts (if using).
        - ○ Serve immediately and enjoy!

Tips:

- Ensure the oil is at the correct temperature (around 350°F/175°C) to ensure the loukoumades cook evenly and become crispy on the outside.
- Loukoumades are best served fresh and warm, as they may lose their crispiness over time.
- Customize your loukoumades by adding different toppings such as powdered sugar, chocolate sauce, or even a sprinkle of sea salt for a modern twist.

Enjoy these irresistible Greek donuts, Loukoumades, as a delightful treat for dessert or a special occasion!

Taramosalata (Fish Roe Dip)

Ingredients:

- 200g (7 oz) tarama (fish roe)
- 1 medium-sized potato, boiled and mashed (or 1 slice of white bread, soaked in water and squeezed dry)
- 1/2 cup olive oil (extra virgin preferred)
- Juice of 1-2 lemons (adjust to taste)
- 1-2 garlic cloves, minced (optional)
- Salt and pepper, to taste
- Water, as needed

Instructions:

1. **Prepare the Tarama:**
   - If using salted tarama, rinse it under cold water and place it in a bowl. Mash it with a fork to break up any large pieces.
2. **Make the Base:**
   - In a food processor or blender, combine the mashed potato (or soaked and squeezed bread) with the tarama and blend until smooth.
3. **Blend with Olive Oil:**
   - With the food processor or blender running, gradually add the olive oil in a steady stream until the mixture is smooth and creamy.
4. **Add Lemon Juice and Seasonings:**
   - Gradually add the lemon juice, minced garlic (if using), salt, and pepper. Blend until well combined.
5. **Adjust Consistency:**
   - If the dip is too thick, add a little water (about 1-2 tablespoons at a time) and blend until you reach your desired consistency.
6. **Chill and Serve:**
   - Transfer the Taramosalata to a bowl and cover it with plastic wrap.
   - Refrigerate for at least 1-2 hours to allow the flavors to meld together.
   - Before serving, garnish with a drizzle of olive oil and a sprinkle of paprika or fresh herbs (optional).

Tips:

- **Tarama Variations:** Depending on personal preference and availability, you can adjust the ratio of tarama to potato (or bread) for a thicker or lighter texture.
- **Storage:** Taramosalata can be stored in an airtight container in the refrigerator for up to 3-4 days. Stir well before serving if any separation occurs.
- **Serving:** Serve Taramosalata chilled with pita bread, crusty bread, or vegetable sticks as an appetizer or part of a meze platter.

Enjoy this creamy and flavorful Taramosalata dip, perfect for sharing during gatherings or as a delicious start to a Greek-inspired meal!

Strapatsada (Scrambled Eggs with Tomatoes)

Ingredients:

- 4-5 large eggs
- 4 medium-sized tomatoes, ripe and chopped
- 1 onion, finely chopped
- 2-3 tbsp olive oil
- 1/2 tsp dried oregano
- Salt and pepper, to taste
- Optional: 50g feta cheese, crumbled (for added creaminess and tang)

Instructions:

1. **Prepare the Tomatoes:**
   - Heat the olive oil in a large skillet or frying pan over medium heat.
   - Add the chopped onion and sauté until softened and translucent, about 3-4 minutes.
   - Add the chopped tomatoes to the skillet, along with a pinch of salt and pepper. Cook for about 8-10 minutes, stirring occasionally, until the tomatoes break down and release their juices.
2. **Scramble the Eggs:**
   - In a bowl, whisk the eggs together with a pinch of salt, pepper, and dried oregano until well combined.
   - Pour the eggs into the skillet with the tomatoes. Gently stir the mixture with a spatula, scraping the bottom of the skillet occasionally to scramble the eggs.
   - Continue cooking and stirring gently until the eggs are cooked to your desired consistency, about 3-5 minutes. The eggs should be creamy and moist.
3. **Optional: Add Feta Cheese:**
   - If using feta cheese, crumble it over the eggs during the last minute of cooking. Stir gently to incorporate the cheese into the eggs.
4. **Serve:**
   - Remove the skillet from heat.
   - Serve the Strapatsada immediately, garnished with fresh herbs like parsley or dill if desired.
   - Enjoy warm, with crusty bread or toast on the side.

Tips:

- **Variations:** You can personalize this dish by adding other ingredients such as chopped bell peppers, spinach, or even a dash of paprika for extra flavor.
- **Herbs:** Fresh herbs like parsley or dill can be sprinkled over the finished dish for added freshness and aroma.

- **Serving:** Strapatsada is often served as a main dish for breakfast or brunch, but it can also be enjoyed as a light lunch or dinner with a side salad.

This Strapatsada recipe captures the essence of Greek comfort food—simple ingredients cooked together to create a satisfying and flavorful dish.

Dakos (Cretan Salad)

Ingredients:

- 2 large ripe tomatoes, diced
- 1 small red onion, thinly sliced
- 1/2 cup Kalamata olives, pitted and sliced
- 200g feta cheese, crumbled
- 4-6 barley rusks (paximadia), or substitute with whole grain rusk or toasted bread slices
- Extra virgin olive oil, for drizzling
- Dried oregano, for sprinkling
- Salt and pepper, to taste

Instructions:

1. **Prepare the Ingredients:**
   - Dice the tomatoes into small pieces. Thinly slice the red onion and pit and slice the Kalamata olives. Crumble the feta cheese.
2. **Assemble the Dakos:**
   - Place the barley rusks (paximadia) on a serving platter or individual plates.
   - Sprinkle the diced tomatoes evenly over the rusks, followed by the sliced red onion and Kalamata olives.
   - Distribute the crumbled feta cheese over the top of each rusk.
3. **Season and Serve:**
   - Drizzle extra virgin olive oil generously over each Dakos.
   - Sprinkle dried oregano, salt, and pepper over the salads according to taste.
4. **Serve Immediately:**
   - Serve Dakos immediately after assembling to enjoy the flavors and textures while the rusks are still slightly crisp.

Tips:

- **Barley Rusks:** If you can't find barley rusks (paximadia), you can substitute with whole grain rusk or toasted bread slices. Traditional Dakos uses the barley rusk for its hearty texture.
- **Customize:** Feel free to add additional ingredients such as capers, cucumbers, or fresh herbs like parsley or basil for added freshness and flavor.
- **Make Ahead:** You can prepare the components of Dakos ahead of time but assemble just before serving to prevent the rusks from becoming too soggy.

Dakos is a refreshing and satisfying salad that makes a perfect appetizer or light meal, showcasing the simple yet robust flavors of the Mediterranean region, particularly from the island of Crete.

Karidopita (Walnut Cake)

Ingredients:

For the Cake:

- 1 cup walnuts, finely chopped
- 1 cup breadcrumbs (from stale bread or use fine bread crumbs)
- 1 cup all-purpose flour
- 1 1/2 tsp baking powder
- 1/2 tsp baking soda
- 1/2 tsp ground cinnamon
- 1/4 tsp ground cloves
- 1/4 tsp ground nutmeg
- Pinch of salt
- 1 cup granulated sugar
- 1 cup Greek yogurt
- 1/2 cup olive oil or vegetable oil
- 3 large eggs
- Zest of 1 orange
- Zest of 1 lemon
- 1/2 cup orange juice (freshly squeezed)
- 1/4 cup brandy or cognac (optional)

For the Syrup:

- 1 cup water
- 1 cup granulated sugar
- 1 cinnamon stick
- Peel of 1 lemon

Instructions:

1. **Prepare the Cake:**
    - Preheat your oven to 350°F (175°C). Grease and flour a 9-inch (23 cm) round cake pan or line it with parchment paper.
    - In a bowl, combine the chopped walnuts, breadcrumbs, flour, baking powder, baking soda, ground cinnamon, ground cloves, ground nutmeg, and salt. Mix well and set aside.
    - In another large bowl, whisk together the sugar, Greek yogurt, olive oil, eggs, orange zest, lemon zest, orange juice, and brandy (if using) until smooth and well combined.
    - Gradually add the dry ingredients to the wet ingredients, mixing until just combined. Do not overmix.
2. **Bake the Cake:**

- Pour the batter into the prepared cake pan and spread it evenly.
- Bake in the preheated oven for 40-45 minutes, or until a toothpick inserted into the center of the cake comes out clean.

3. **Prepare the Syrup:**
   - While the cake is baking, prepare the syrup. In a saucepan, combine the water, sugar, cinnamon stick, and lemon peel.
   - Bring the mixture to a boil over medium-high heat, stirring occasionally, until the sugar is completely dissolved.
   - Reduce the heat to low and simmer for 5 minutes. Remove from heat and let the syrup cool slightly. Discard the cinnamon stick and lemon peel.

4. **Soak the Cake:**
   - Once the cake is baked and while it's still warm, use a skewer or fork to poke holes all over the top of the cake.
   - Slowly pour the warm syrup over the warm cake, allowing it to absorb the syrup. Let the cake cool completely in the pan.

5. **Serve:**
   - Once cooled, carefully remove the cake from the pan and transfer it to a serving platter.
   - Slice and serve the Karidopita, optionally garnishing with additional chopped walnuts or a dusting of powdered sugar.

Tips:

- **Storage:** Karidopita can be stored at room temperature, covered, for a few days. The syrup helps keep it moist.
- **Variations:** Some recipes include adding cloves or other spices, adjusting to personal taste preferences.
- **Serve:** Enjoy Karidopita with a cup of Greek coffee or tea as a delightful dessert or treat.

This recipe captures the essence of Karidopita—a moist and flavorful walnut cake soaked in a sweet syrup, perfect for sharing at gatherings or enjoying as a special dessert.

Souvlakia (Skewers with Lamb or Chicken)

Ingredients:

For the Marinade:

- 1/4 cup olive oil
- Juice of 1 lemon
- 3 garlic cloves, minced
- 1 tsp dried oregano
- 1 tsp dried thyme
- 1/2 tsp paprika
- Salt and pepper, to taste

For the Skewers:

- 1 lb (450g) lamb or chicken breast, cut into 1-inch cubes
- Wooden or metal skewers (if using wooden, soak them in water for 30 minutes before using)

For Serving:

- Pita bread
- Tzatziki sauce (see recipe below)
- Chopped tomatoes, cucumbers, red onions (for salad)
- Lemon wedges

Instructions:

1. **Prepare the Marinade:**
    - In a bowl, whisk together the olive oil, lemon juice, minced garlic, dried oregano, dried thyme, paprika, salt, and pepper.
2. **Marinate the Meat:**
    - Place the cubed lamb or chicken in a shallow dish or resealable plastic bag.
    - Pour the marinade over the meat, making sure it is evenly coated. Cover the dish or seal the bag, and refrigerate for at least 1 hour, preferably longer (up to overnight) to allow the flavors to meld.
3. **Skewer the Meat:**
    - If using wooden skewers, thread the marinated meat onto the skewers, leaving a little space between each piece.
4. **Grill the Souvlakia:**
    - Preheat your grill or grill pan over medium-high heat.
    - Grill the skewers for about 8-10 minutes, turning occasionally, until the meat is cooked through and nicely charred on all sides.
5. **Prepare Tzatziki Sauce:**

- While the meat is grilling, prepare the tzatziki sauce if not already made (see recipe below).
6. **Serve:**
    - Serve the Souvlakia hot off the grill with pita bread, tzatziki sauce, and a side of chopped tomatoes, cucumbers, and red onions.
    - Squeeze fresh lemon juice over the skewers before serving for added zestiness.

Tzatziki Sauce Recipe:

- 1 cup Greek yogurt
- 1 cucumber, grated and excess water squeezed out
- 2 cloves garlic, minced
- 1 tbsp olive oil
- 1 tbsp lemon juice
- 1 tbsp chopped fresh dill (or mint)
- Salt and pepper, to taste
    1. In a bowl, combine the Greek yogurt, grated cucumber, minced garlic, olive oil, lemon juice, chopped fresh dill (or mint), salt, and pepper.
    2. Mix well until all ingredients are incorporated.
    3. Refrigerate for at least 30 minutes to allow the flavors to meld together before serving.

Tips:

- **Variations:** You can add bell peppers, onions, or cherry tomatoes to the skewers for added flavor and color.
- **Grilling:** Ensure your grill or grill pan is hot before adding the skewers to get a nice sear on the meat.
- **Serving:** Souvlakia are traditionally served with pita bread and tzatziki sauce, but you can also enjoy them with a Greek salad or grilled vegetables.

Enjoy these delicious Greek Souvlakia skewers with your favorite sides for a taste of Mediterranean flavors at home!

Moussaka (Eggplant Casserole)

Ingredients:

For the Eggplant Layers:

- 2-3 large eggplants, sliced lengthwise into 1/4-inch thick slices
- Salt, for sprinkling
- Olive oil, for brushing

For the Meat Sauce:

- 1 lb (450g) ground lamb or beef
- 1 onion, finely chopped
- 2-3 garlic cloves, minced
- 1 can (14 oz) diced tomatoes
- 2 tbsp tomato paste
- 1 tsp dried oregano
- 1/2 tsp ground cinnamon
- Salt and pepper, to taste
- Olive oil, for cooking

For the Béchamel Sauce:

- 1/2 cup unsalted butter
- 1/2 cup all-purpose flour
- 4 cups milk
- 1/4 tsp ground nutmeg
- Salt and pepper, to taste
- 2 large eggs, lightly beaten
- 1/2 cup grated Parmesan cheese

For Assembly:

- Olive oil, for greasing
- 1/2 cup grated Parmesan cheese, for topping
- Fresh parsley, chopped (optional, for garnish)

Instructions:

1. **Prepare the Eggplant:**
    - Place the eggplant slices on a baking sheet and sprinkle both sides with salt. Let them sit for about 30 minutes to release bitterness.
    - Preheat your oven to 400°F (200°C). Rinse the eggplant slices under cold water and pat them dry with paper towels. Brush both sides lightly with olive oil.

- Arrange the eggplant slices on baking sheets and bake for 15-20 minutes, flipping halfway through, until tender and lightly browned. Remove from the oven and set aside.

2. **Make the Meat Sauce:**
   - In a large skillet or frying pan, heat olive oil over medium-high heat. Add the chopped onion and sauté until softened and translucent, about 5 minutes.
   - Add the minced garlic and cook for another minute until fragrant.
   - Add the ground lamb or beef to the skillet, breaking it up with a spoon. Cook until browned and cooked through, about 5-7 minutes.
   - Stir in the diced tomatoes, tomato paste, dried oregano, ground cinnamon, salt, and pepper. Simmer for 15-20 minutes, stirring occasionally, until the sauce has thickened. Remove from heat and set aside.

3. **Make the Béchamel Sauce:**
   - In a large saucepan, melt the butter over medium heat. Once melted, add the flour and whisk continuously for 1-2 minutes to cook the flour and form a roux.
   - Gradually add the milk to the roux, whisking constantly to prevent lumps from forming.
   - Cook the sauce, stirring constantly, until it thickens and comes to a simmer. Reduce heat to low and cook for another 2-3 minutes until smooth and creamy.
   - Remove the saucepan from heat and stir in the ground nutmeg, salt, and pepper.
   - Allow the béchamel sauce to cool slightly, then gradually whisk in the lightly beaten eggs and grated Parmesan cheese until well combined.

4. **Assemble the Moussaka:**
   - Preheat your oven to 375°F (190°C). Grease a large baking dish (about 9x13 inches) with olive oil.
   - Arrange half of the baked eggplant slices in a single layer on the bottom of the baking dish.
   - Spread half of the meat sauce evenly over the eggplant layer.
   - Add another layer of the remaining eggplant slices, followed by the rest of the meat sauce.
   - Pour the béchamel sauce over the top, spreading it evenly with a spatula to cover the entire surface.
   - Sprinkle the grated Parmesan cheese evenly over the béchamel sauce.

5. **Bake the Moussaka:**
   - Place the assembled moussaka in the preheated oven and bake for 45-55 minutes, or until the top is golden brown and bubbly.
   - Remove from the oven and let it cool for 10-15 minutes before slicing and serving.

6. **Serve:**
   - Garnish the moussaka with chopped fresh parsley (if using) and serve warm.

Tips:

- **Eggplant Preparation:** Salting and baking the eggplant slices helps remove bitterness and excess moisture, ensuring a tender texture in the moussaka.
- **Make Ahead:** Moussaka can be assembled ahead of time and refrigerated before baking. This allows flavors to meld even more, making it a great dish for entertaining.
- **Storage:** Leftover moussaka can be stored in an airtight container in the refrigerator for 3-4 days. Reheat in the oven or microwave before serving.

Enjoy this hearty and flavorful Greek moussaka, perfect for a comforting meal with family and friends!

Spanakopita (Spinach Pie)

Ingredients:

For the Filling:

- 1 lb (450g) fresh spinach, washed and chopped (or 10 oz frozen spinach, thawed and drained)
- 1 bunch green onions (about 5-6), finely chopped
- 1 small onion, finely chopped
- 2-3 cloves garlic, minced
- 1/2 cup fresh dill, chopped (or 2 tbsp dried dill)
- 1/2 cup fresh parsley, chopped
- 8 oz (225g) feta cheese, crumbled
- 4 oz (115g) ricotta cheese (or cottage cheese)
- 3 eggs
- Salt and pepper, to taste
- Olive oil, for sautéing

For the Phyllo Layers:

- 1/2 lb (about 20 sheets) phyllo dough, thawed if frozen
- 1/2 cup unsalted butter, melted (or olive oil)

Instructions:

1. **Prepare the Filling:**
    - If using fresh spinach, wash and chop it. If using frozen spinach, make sure it's thawed and well-drained.
    - In a large skillet, heat a drizzle of olive oil over medium heat. Add the chopped green onions and onion, and sauté until softened, about 3-4 minutes.
    - Add the minced garlic and sauté for another minute until fragrant.
    - Add the chopped spinach to the skillet in batches, allowing it to wilt down. Cook for 2-3 minutes until the spinach is tender and any excess liquid has evaporated.
    - Remove the skillet from heat and let the mixture cool slightly.
    - In a large bowl, combine the cooked spinach mixture with chopped dill, parsley, crumbled feta cheese, ricotta (or cottage cheese), and eggs. Mix well to combine. Season with salt and pepper to taste.
2. **Assemble the Spanakopita:**
    - Preheat your oven to 375°F (190°C). Lightly grease a 9x13 inch baking dish with olive oil or butter.
    - Unroll the phyllo dough and cover it with a damp kitchen towel to prevent it from drying out.

- Place one sheet of phyllo dough in the prepared baking dish and brush it lightly with melted butter or olive oil. Repeat with 7-8 more sheets, layering them and brushing each sheet with butter or oil.
- Spread the spinach and cheese mixture evenly over the phyllo layers in the dish.
- Continue layering the remaining phyllo sheets on top of the spinach mixture, brushing each sheet with butter or oil.

3. **Bake the Spanakopita:**
    - Using a sharp knife, carefully score the top layers of phyllo into squares or diamonds, being careful not to cut all the way through to the bottom.
    - Bake in the preheated oven for 45-50 minutes, or until the top is golden brown and crisp.
4. **Serve:**
    - Remove from the oven and let it cool for a few minutes before slicing along the scored lines and serving warm.

Tips:

- **Phyllo Dough Handling:** Phyllo dough dries out quickly, so work efficiently and keep it covered with a damp cloth while assembling the pie.
- **Variations:** You can add other ingredients such as pine nuts, mint, or a squeeze of lemon juice to the spinach filling for additional flavor.
- **Make Ahead:** Spanakopita can be assembled ahead of time and refrigerated (unbaked) until ready to bake. This makes it a convenient dish for parties or gatherings.

Spanakopita is best enjoyed fresh and warm, but leftovers can be stored in an airtight container in the refrigerator for a few days. Reheat in the oven to crisp up the phyllo layers before serving again. Enjoy this savory Greek spinach pie as a delightful appetizer or main dish!

Avgolemono (Egg-Lemon Chicken Soup)

Ingredients:

- 6 cups chicken broth (homemade or low-sodium store-bought)
- 1/2 cup Arborio rice or long-grain rice
- 2 boneless, skinless chicken breasts (about 1 lb), cooked and shredded (optional)
- 2 large eggs
- Juice of 2 lemons (about 1/2 cup)
- Salt and pepper, to taste
- Fresh dill, chopped (optional, for garnish)

Instructions:

1. **Cook the Rice:**
    - In a large pot, bring the chicken broth to a boil over medium-high heat.
    - Add the rice to the boiling broth and reduce heat to medium-low. Simmer, uncovered, for about 15-20 minutes, or until the rice is cooked through and tender.
    - If using shredded chicken, add it to the pot during the last 5 minutes of cooking to heat through.
2. **Prepare the Avgolemono Mixture:**
    - While the rice is cooking, prepare the Avgolemono sauce. In a medium bowl, whisk together the eggs and lemon juice until smooth and frothy.
3. **Temper the Eggs:**
    - Once the rice (and chicken, if using) is cooked, reduce the heat to low.
    - Take about 1 cup of hot broth from the pot and slowly pour it into the egg-lemon mixture, whisking constantly to prevent the eggs from curdling.
    - Gradually add another cup of hot broth to the egg-lemon mixture, continuing to whisk until well combined.
4. **Combine and Serve:**
    - Pour the egg-lemon mixture back into the pot with the rice and broth, stirring gently to combine. The heat from the broth will cook the eggs and thicken the soup.
    - Season with salt and pepper to taste. Be cautious with the salt as the broth might already be seasoned.
5. **Serve:**
    - Ladle the Avgolemono soup into bowls and garnish with chopped fresh dill, if desired.
    - Serve hot, with crusty bread on the side if desired.

Tips:

- **Consistency:** If the soup is too thick for your liking, you can thin it out with a bit of hot broth or water.
- **Chicken:** The shredded chicken is optional but adds extra heartiness to the soup. You can also use leftover cooked chicken or rotisserie chicken for convenience.
- **Reheating:** Avgolemono soup can be reheated gently over low heat to avoid curdling the eggs. Stir well before serving.
- **Variations:** Some recipes include adding a bay leaf or a pinch of nutmeg for additional flavor complexity.

Avgolemono soup is a delicious and comforting dish that showcases the delicate balance of tangy lemon and creamy egg. It's a staple in Greek cuisine and is sure to warm you up on a chilly day or whenever you need a comforting bowl of soup.

Fasolada (Bean Soup)

Ingredients:

- 1 cup dried white beans (such as Great Northern beans or cannellini beans), soaked overnight
- 2-3 tbsp olive oil
- 1 onion, finely chopped
- 2 carrots, diced
- 2 celery stalks, diced
- 3 garlic cloves, minced
- 1 can (14 oz) diced tomatoes
- 1 bay leaf
- 1 tsp dried oregano
- Salt and pepper, to taste
- 6 cups vegetable or chicken broth (or water)
- Fresh parsley, chopped (for garnish)
- Lemon wedges (for serving)

Instructions:

1. **Prepare the Beans:**
    - Rinse the soaked beans under cold water and drain.
2. **Cook the Soup:**
    - In a large pot, heat the olive oil over medium heat. Add the chopped onion, carrots, and celery. Sauté for 5-7 minutes, until the vegetables are softened and the onion is translucent.
    - Add the minced garlic and cook for another minute until fragrant.
    - Stir in the diced tomatoes, bay leaf, dried oregano, salt, and pepper. Cook for 2-3 minutes, stirring occasionally.
    - Add the soaked beans to the pot and pour in the vegetable or chicken broth (or water), ensuring that the beans are covered by about an inch of liquid.
    - Bring the soup to a boil, then reduce the heat to low. Cover and simmer gently for 1.5 to 2 hours, or until the beans are tender and cooked through. Stir occasionally and skim off any foam that may form on the surface.
3. **Finish the Soup:**
    - Once the beans are tender, taste the soup and adjust seasoning with more salt and pepper if needed.
    - Remove the bay leaf from the soup and discard.
4. **Serve:**
    - Ladle the Fasolada into bowls and garnish with chopped fresh parsley.
    - Serve hot, with a wedge of lemon on the side for squeezing over the soup before eating.

Tips:

- **Variations:** Some recipes may include additional vegetables like potatoes or bell peppers. You can also add a splash of red wine vinegar or a dollop of Greek yogurt to enhance the flavors.
- **Storage:** Fasolada keeps well and often tastes even better the next day after flavors have had time to meld. Store any leftovers in an airtight container in the refrigerator for up to 4-5 days.
- **Serve with:** Fasolada is traditionally served with crusty bread or a slice of country-style bread for dipping.

Fasolada is not only delicious but also nutritious, making it a perfect meal option for vegetarians and anyone looking to enjoy a hearty, comforting soup.

Baklava

Ingredients:

For the Baklava:

- 1 package (16 oz) phyllo dough, thawed if frozen
- 1 1/2 cups mixed nuts (such as walnuts, pistachios, almonds), finely chopped
- 1 cup unsalted butter, melted
- 1/2 cup granulated sugar
- 1 tsp ground cinnamon
- 1/4 tsp ground cloves

For the Syrup:

- 1 cup water
- 1 cup granulated sugar
- 1/2 cup honey
- 1 cinnamon stick
- 3-4 whole cloves
- 1 strip of lemon peel

Instructions:

1. **Prepare the Syrup:**
    - In a saucepan, combine water, sugar, honey, cinnamon stick, whole cloves, and lemon peel.
    - Bring the mixture to a boil over medium-high heat, stirring occasionally to dissolve the sugar. Reduce the heat to low and simmer for about 10 minutes. Remove from heat and let it cool completely. Once cooled, remove the cinnamon stick, cloves, and lemon peel.
2. **Prepare the Baklava:**
    - Preheat your oven to 350°F (175°C). Grease a 9x13 inch baking dish with butter.
    - In a bowl, combine the finely chopped nuts with granulated sugar, ground cinnamon, and ground cloves. Mix well and set aside.
    - Unroll the phyllo dough and place it on a clean, dry surface. Cover it with a damp kitchen towel to prevent it from drying out.
    - Brush the bottom of the baking dish with melted butter. Place one sheet of phyllo dough in the dish and brush it with melted butter. Repeat with about 8-10 sheets of phyllo, brushing each sheet with butter before adding the next.
    - Sprinkle a thin, even layer of the nut mixture over the top of the buttered phyllo layers.
    - Continue layering the phyllo sheets and butter, alternating with layers of the nut mixture, until all the nuts are used, ending with a top layer of phyllo dough. Brush the top layer generously with melted butter.

3. **Cut and Bake:**
   - Using a sharp knife, cut the baklava into diamond or square-shaped pieces, cutting all the way through the layers.
   - Place the baking dish in the preheated oven and bake for 45-50 minutes, or until the baklava is golden brown and crisp.
4. **Finish and Serve:**
   - Remove the baklava from the oven and immediately pour the cooled syrup evenly over the hot baklava, allowing it to soak in completely.
   - Let the baklava cool completely in the dish on a wire rack. This allows the flavors to meld and the syrup to absorb fully.
   - Once cooled, carefully remove the pieces of baklava from the dish and serve on a platter. Enjoy this delicious dessert with a cup of Greek coffee or tea!

Tips:

- **Handling Phyllo Dough:** Phyllo dough is delicate and dries out quickly. Keep it covered with a damp towel while working with it to prevent it from becoming brittle.
- **Nuts:** You can customize the nut mixture according to your preference or what you have available. Traditional baklava often includes a mix of walnuts, pistachios, and almonds.
- **Storage:** Store leftover baklava in an airtight container at room temperature for up to a week. The flavors often improve as it sits.

Baklava is a labor of love but well worth the effort for its rich flavors and delicate, flaky texture. It's a perfect dessert to impress guests or enjoy as a special treat for yourself!

www.ingramcontent.com/pod-product-compliance
Lightning Source LLC
LaVergne TN
LVHW081604060526
838201LV00054B/2074